Misdiagnosed

The Search for Dr. House

Author: Nika C. Beamon

Copyright 2014

ISBN: 978-1500436674

Advanced Praise for Misdiagnosed:

"MISDIAGNOSED is an eye-opening, fascinating account of a brave journey through the labyrinth of American medicine. Beamon draws the reader in skillfully, and gives us a close up view of the power of human persistence."

Marya Hornbacher
Hornbacher is a Pulitzer Prize and Pushcart Prize nominated author. Her bestselling books include: Wasted: A Memoir of Anorexia and Bulimia; Madness: A Bi-Polar Life and Waiting: A Non-Believer's Guide to a Higher Power.

"How long can my body endure all the invasions by doctors?" Nika Beamon's cry is heard throughout *Misdiagnosed:* The Search for Dr. House. That doc does not exist, of course, but the author's journey across hazardous terrain in the medical jungle did. Her misery being mangled by modern medicine provides lessons on arming ourselves for the battles many of us face."

Richard M. Cohen is the *New York Times* Best Selling author of *Blindsided* and *Strong at the Broken Places.*

"This is a book is a "must read" for all doctors and healthcare professionals. It details the quest from the perspective of a patient for a diagnosis suffering from non-descript complaints that typify the autoimmune diseases. Enigmatic to most physicians, devastating to patients, the stuff of science fiction, and limitless in presentation; autoimmune diseases are the frontier of medicine in the 21st century. They demand an understanding of complex science and while practicing the art of medicine with compassion. Nika seeks answers from learned doctors while her personal and physical life crumbles around her. Read her story to understand why patients long for a diagnosis."

Robert G. Lahita MD, PhD, FACP, MACR, FRCP Chairman of Medicine and VP, Newark Beth Israel Medical Center, Professor of Medicine, UMDNJ

"Misdiagnosed" is a gripping medical detective story. It could be a fictional episode of "House" from the patient's perspective, but this story is real. It is a raw telling of Nika Beamon's journey through high-tech American health care. Just as she recounts stripping naked for doctors' probes and surgeons' scalpels, Beamon bares hers physical and emotional tribulations to readers."

Andrew Holtz, MPH

Author, The Medical Science of House, M.D.

Author, House, M.D. vs. Reality

Author, The Real Grey's Anatomy

"Nika's book is a well written, eye opening, call to action. An inspiring, yet alarming story that lets us know that even in our darkest and most alone moments, that we are not alone."

Wes Moore

Bestselling author, "The Other Wes Moore."

"This long-overdue book overcomes a long tradition of silence and isolation for women with misdiagnosed and rare illnesses, especially for African American women. But everyone with an invisible illness, whether named or not, will relate to Nika Beamon's hidden dramas in her life, dealing with the daily frustrations of a mysteriously uncooperative body -- and then, often worse, with an ill-equipped, punishing medical system. Written with the intimacy and boldness of a conversation among best girlfriends, she fearlessly portrays the heartaches of living with a little understood and rare immune disorder, and how it affects every area of her life."

Paula Kamen

Author of All in My Head: An Epic Quest to Cure an Unrelenting, Totally Unreasonable, and Only Slightly Enlightening Headache

'I read "Misdiagnosed" and just wanted to share with you that I love it! It is well written, fiesty, and witty, while managing to capture the seriousness of the situation and all the emotions that go into it. I will definitely tell my friends and family to buy it."

Nicoletta Skoufalos, Ph.D.

Licensed Clinical Psychologist

"As the Health Communications Manager at the National Women's Health Network, and having spent 5 years working for the National Women's Health Information Center, a contract sponsored by the Department of Health and Human Services Office on Women's Health, Nika's story was all too familiar...

Hearing about the ups and downs of your relationship with Bryce really drew me in and not only made it a medical drama but a love drama as well...

It took you almost two decades to finally figure out what was going on with you. Most people would have given up and just succumbed to their illness. But to see you take your health care in to your hands and continue to fight for what you felt was the right diagnosis was truly amazing.

I believe it will truly help someone as they are on the quest for their own. More people need to realize that doctors truly don't know everything and that doctors can be learning about a patient's illness right along with them!"

Shaniqua D. Seth
Health Communications Manager
National Women's Health Network

"Why Beamon's Misdiagnosed is a must read:

- Misdiagnosed sheds light the experiences of African American and other minorities who have a well-documented history of getting substandard or inadequate medical treatment in the U.S. A research study cited in a February 14, 2010 *Daily Beast* article said "race-related differences in health care cost the country 229 billion between 2003 and 2006" alone; a fact that "Health and Human Services Secretary Kathleen Sebelius called 'just stunning and shocking.'"

- Misdiagnosed serves a cautionary guide to anyone who falls ill or has a loved one suffering with an ailment in the US. A recent John Hopkins study found that hospital errors lead to as many as 40,500 patients dying annually... These mistakes cost nearly one third of the 2.7 trillion spent in the

US on healthcare. A study published in April
showed one in every 20 people or 12 million per
year are misdiagnosed at outpatient clinics in the
U.S."

Yvette Caslin
RollingOut.Com

This book is dedicated to all those who like me know:

Illness may temporarily reign over my body but I, along with God, am the 'captain of my soul.' I am loved. I've been loved. I have more love to give so I cannot and will not surrender.

DISCLOSURE:

The names of certain characters have been changed to protect the privacy of some people in the book.

Additionally, this book is not intended as a substitute for the medical advice of physicians. The reader should regularly consult a physician in matters relating to his/her health and particularly with respect to any symptoms that may require diagnosis or medical attention.

Table of Contents:

Preface:
Freak of Nature

I am a "freak of nature." I have a condition few others in the world share, but at least I know that now. I spent the better part of my twenties and all of my thirties, which should've been my carefree years, trying to find someone to tell me what was wrong with my body. In 2004, I was so desperate I began watching the TV show *House M.D.*, hoping it could help. I tuned in every week not to see how Dr. Gregory House would misbehave but to see whom he'd be treating, if he'd have a case like mine. It never happened; I never saw anyone with the exact same symptoms. I was disappointed but not surprised. By this time, I'd already struggled for eleven years to find an answer about what ailed me.

My life changed dramatically my senior year at Boston College in Massachusetts in 1993. I'd planned to spend it partying with my friends and enjoying the spoils of my hard work trying to earn a dual degree in communications and sociology. I never got to do that. I began suffering a rash of 104-degree fevers, joint pain, and debilitating fatigue that made it impossible for me to make it to class most days. I adjusted: I had my assignments brought to me in my room, sitting a Mac on my lap to type papers, and I had friends over instead of going out. I didn't know it then, but it was just the beginning of the changes I'd have to make in my life.

At first I endured minor inconveniences, like a few days bedridden each month, a doctor's appointment every two weeks, and a couple of pills. These weren't things that prevented me from beginning a demanding career in television, which required working long hours and some weekends. I was able to focus on learning all aspects of the business, including writing and production. I also had the energy to join a softball team, volunteer for charity sports tournaments, and spend time with my boyfriend.
A few years later, my body began to decline rapidly. Right after I broke up with my boyfriend, moved back home to the New York–New Jersey area without a job, and started writing my first book, my aches, pains, and
fatigue made it nearly impossible for me to concentrate on anything, let alone get out and look for a job. I was quickly

depleting my savings, and I had no health insurance. It was the first time my failing health made me wonder what kind of future I'd have, especially on my own.

My symptoms soon eased, though, and I was able to take a job at Classic Sports Network, which became ESPN Classic, in New York. As HR/office manager, I was pretty sedentary, saving my energy for activities after work, such as finishing my novel and jumping back into the dating scene. I thought I'd found a way around the nagging condition that had slowed me down, but I'd only paused it.

It took four more years for me to realize I wasn't in control of my body at all. A stabbing pain in my abdomen greeted me as I stepped inside the *Eyewitness News* office in New York for the first time, on April 20, 1999. I was concerned but didn't have time to deal with it. The newsroom was bustling. People were running around, shouting and cussing. I'd come in just moments after word had spread about the Columbine High School massacre.

I scurried into a chair and tried to shake off the pain while maintaining a professional exterior. Good thing I collected myself, because within minutes, my new boss, who had failed to reintroduce himself, was asking me to make travel arrangements for a reporter and cameraperson.

"Welcome, Nika," he said. "I hope you are settled in. I need you to book two tickets to Denver, Colorado, for Nelson Gregg and Steven Sharp."

Who? I thought but didn't ask.

"They need to get there as soon as possible."

"Is there a return date?"

"No, not right now," he barked. "They will also need a car and a hotel, though."

I didn't even know how to use the phone, but I quickly figured it out. I dialed the number for ABC Travel, mounted on the wall above the phone, and prayed the person on the other end knew the crucial details, like how to pay for the tickets and hotel.

"Joanna speaking. How can I help you?" the voice on the other end of the line said.

"This is Nika Beamon from WABC-TV. I need to get two tickets to Colorado as soon as possible."

"No problem. Let me tell you what your options are."

Joanna rattled off the possible flights and helped me select the best one for the station's crew.

"Did you need a car and a hotel booked for them as well?" she asked.

"Yes, please."

It took less than fifteen minutes for me to complete my first task as the new newsroom manager at the number-one local-television station in the country. I did it without letting on that the pain in my gut made me want to double over.

This is only half the job, I thought, as I rubbed my abdomen with a fake smile plastered on my face. I had also agreed to produce a live sports segment on Friday mornings at 4:00 AM. *I wonder how I'm going to pull this off.*

The demands of my career took a toll on my frail body very quickly. A mere year and a half into my job at *Eyewitness News*, I was spending less and less time going out after work. It was all I could do most days to make it through my nine-hour shift without needing to take one of the pain pills my doctors had begun prescribing. As my symptoms progressed, my primary care physician suggested various specialists across the city, each focused on one aspect of what was going wrong with me. Instead of hanging out at clubs, I was lying on my back in hospital rooms and on exam tables, hoping someone could help me. Meeting men so I could occasionally go on a date was out of the question, not just because of my physical limitations but because I dreaded the thought of trying to explain to someone that I was stricken with some mysterious illness that appeared to have no cure. So I turned my attention to answering these questions for myself.

I drove countless miles to meet a slew of strange doctors. I endured colonoscopies to check my intestines, endoscopies to examine my throat and stomach, and biopsies to search my organs for cancer. I had a spinal tap to look for infection, a transesophageal echocardiogram to make sure

my heart was strong, and countless blood and urine tests. I also had enough radiation that my insides probably still glow in the dark. But I had no choice. At the time, I was told if I wanted to figure out what was going on inside me, all of these exams were necessary.

A lot of the doctors admitted they were as baffled as I by my case. Most agreed that my liver was damaged, my colon and intestines were inflamed, polyps blocked my ovaries, and my lymph nodes were constantly swollen. However, no one knew of just one condition that covered all my symptoms. I had MRIs, CAT scans, and every other kind of test the doctors could order to try to narrow down the cause of my illness. When those didn't work, I was sent to just about every kind of "ologist" that exists: a hematologist to check my blood, an endocrinologist to check my hormone levels, a dermatologist to check for skin cancer, a cardiologist to check my heart, a rheumatologist to check my joints and figure out the cause of my fevers, an immunologist to make sure my body could fight infections, a neurologist to check the blood vessels in my neck and brain for clots and other defects, and a radiologist to examine the images of my organs.

As the list of specialists grew, my list of medications increased as well. Unfortunately, most of the drugs I was on had no street value, so I couldn't even sell them to make back the fortune in hard-earned cash I shelled out for them. To cover the cost, I skipped vacations, new clothes and furniture, dinners out, and even holiday presents. Just trying to keep track of my refills or which doctor prescribed what drugs required an Excel spreadsheet. My doctors often thought they'd solved my case. They diagnosed me with numerous conditions over the years, some of which I'm sure I never really had, including mononucleosis; chronic fatigue syndrome; acid reflux disease, or GERD, so severe it eroded my esophagus; polycystic ovary syndrome, a hormone imbalance causing cysts, fertility and menstruation problems, and excess hair growth; acanthosis nigricans, a skin disorder that can be a sign of cancer; insulin resistance syndrome, a metabolic syndrome that can increase the likelihood of coronary artery disease, stroke, and type 2 diabetes; nonalcoholic fatty liver disease, an inflammation of the liver caused by an accumulation of fat deposits; transient ischemic attacks, disruptions of blood flow to the brain; sarcoidosis, a condition that forms abnormal tissue in various organs; and lymphoma, a type of cancer.

Over the course of my medical odyssey, I did manage to find someone who wanted to be with me, illness and all. Nothing about my first date with Bryce went well. In fact, it ended in the hospital. Yet he asked me out again and again, until we ended up spending more than a decade together. He went to doctor's appointments, cleaned up after me, and acted as my eyes, hands, and legs when mine failed.

Still, my years of being half dead didn't affect only me; they also took a toll on him—and on nearly everyone else in my world. Each misdiagnosis was another crushing blow and another affirmation that I might never be cured. Bryce, like my parents and friends, tried to take it well, but he was always in a precarious position: caring for and about me but wanting the normalcy that every couple should have. At first he stayed home with me at night, even though I fell asleep at nine o'clock. But slowly he began going out without me, and our lives started to drift apart.

I didn't blame him. I figured he wondered, like I did, why a healthy, attractive, single man in his twenties would want to be shackled to a girlfriend puking or passing out all the time, and not because of alcohol; why he'd want to be in bed every Friday and Saturday night just after the sun went down, especially when it was not to have sex; and what kind of future we would have, when mine was so unclear. I understood the frustration he must've felt, because I experienced it too. I wanted to be able to go out for a drink, but I knew it would interfere with my medication. I wanted to go dancing with him, but my body hurt just walking. I wanted to see the world with him, but I could barely afford to keep a roof over my head. So when it became apparent none of these things was going to be possible, I wasn't surprised when he found other women he could enjoy and that he and I weren't going to make it. Still, I felt fortunate that he had loved me enough to care for me when I needed him most, and that we could salvage a friendship.

When it comes to my other friends, I know the ones who are still standing after years of get-well cards, calls, and visits are the ones who truly didn't tire of asking the same questions so many times: What did the doctor say? How did your test go? How do you feel? Is there anything I can do?

My parents never asked how they could help; they just rallied around me and figured it out. I have no idea what they expected my life to be like when they stood proudly behind me at my college graduation and sent me out into the world. If my conditions made me fall short, they never said so. They never asked for grandchildren after they knew it would be nearly impossible for me to have them. They never asked if I would get married. When I met a new love interest, they only asked if I found someone who made me happy.

They never complained about traveling to hospitals in three different states repeatedly. They also never seemed to panic whenever I fell ill, nor did they allow me to give in to the depression and doubt that often overwhelmed me. They were, and are, the picture of strength, having always remained positive about my prognosis even when we didn't know how accurate it was. They only ever asked one thing of me: that I not let my condition stop me from accomplishing my goals.

One of the key things I wanted to achieve was a sense of normalcy amid the unpredictability of my infirmity. That's why my coworkers, by far the people I've spent the most time with, were oblivious to what I was going through. I didn't want their looks of pity every day, so I hid my growing dependence on prescription drugs, the severity of my pain, and my endless fatigue from them as best I could.

Plus, I didn't want anyone to break stride, miss their story slot, or even lighten the workload for me. I didn't want my bouts with poor health to make an internal email chain like the one several of our reporters who battled cancer were on. I most certainly didn't want my illness, treatment, or recovery to become the subject of a story designed to boost ratings.

I wanted to report the news, not be it. I succeeded in keeping my private life secret until my illness ravaged my body to the point where it was obvious I was ailing.

Thankfully, by the time I was exposed at work, I'd found a real-life Dr. House, a physician who was able to pinpoint exactly what was wrong with me. It may have taken two decades, but it was worth the wait. Of course, I didn't think that at first. Everyone said I should be glad, happy, relieved—pick your own adjective—to finally know what was wrong with me. But initially I thought, *fuck that.*

It took time for me to realize that the news I'd received lifted a huge burden off my shoulders. No longer did I have to scour online message boards, looking for someone else who shared my symptoms. I didn't have to visit random doctors, looking for a miracle cure. And my family and friends didn't have to be on edge all the time anymore, constantly wondering what bizarre condition I'd be diagnosed with next. We finally knew what I was up against, albeit a rare, incurable disease.

I am a "freak of nature," but I know now it's not a curse. I am as God made me. I have an imperfect body but a strong will. I have determination to make the best of the life He intended for me, even if it's not the one I planned.

Chapter 1: CSI: Jersey City

I'd made much harder decisions than this one—decisions that affected whether I lived or died. Yet I struggled to make up my mind about having a one-night stand.

"So, what's the verdict?" Bryce asked.

I didn't answer. The subway car was so packed with people, I could barely see him, and I certainly didn't think he would even hear me if I responded.

He'd given me an ultimatum: decide whether or not I was going home with him by the time the 1 train reached Times Square, or he would rescind his offer.

When Bryce made the proposition, we were in a bar with our coworkers. It caught me completely off-guard. Until that night, I had known him only from work. I was supposed to be going out for as long as it took for everyone to have a couple of drinks, staying maybe an hour or two at Jake's Dilemma. One hour quickly turned into two, then three. Before I knew it, it was nine o'clock, the time I usually headed home because my medication schedule required that I eat, drug myself, and take a nap, in that order. The rigid timetable often made me turn down

invitations to hang out, but my friend Catherine had begged me to join her as she took Bryce out for a belated birthday celebration. I hadn't been able to refuse her. I'd declined too many times before, blaming my trek to my parents' home in Westchester County, where I was living, for my inability to go out, rather than telling the truth about my failing health.

I did wonder if I'd have a good time out with her, Bryce, his friend, and two other coworkers I was less familiar with, especially since I didn't drink. However, it was the idea of spending time with Bryce that made me most leery. He'd already crossed the line with me one time, about a month earlier, when we had gone to lunch with Catherine. I wasn't offended by his remarks; I was just unnerved by them.

Bryce, Catherine, and I had walked the short distance to the revolving door leading to the company cafeteria, talking about how each of us had made it to the top local TV station in the U.S.

"I came from ESPN," Bryce said.

"Really?" I asked. "I used to work for ESPN Classic."

"When were you there?" Bryce queried.

"I was there from '96 to '99," I responded.

"In '96 I was just graduating from college."

I wasn't sure if he was just sharing or deliberately pointing out that I was at least four years older than he was.

He's the same age as my little brother, I thought, *and I wouldn't date any of his friends, so I should probably stop checking this guy out.*

I couldn't help it, though. I tried to slyly look him up and down as we waited at the grill counter for our turkey burgers and fries to be done. Then I deliberately dropped a few paces behind him as we carried our trays over to a booth in the rear of the cafeteria.

Bryce walked confidently in front of me, seemingly unaware that I was watching. His broad shoulders atop a six-foot-two, mahogany-complexioned frame were undeniably attractive to me. Invisible-rimmed glasses sat firmly on his broad, straight nose, snuggled up next to his long, curly black eyelashes. He was dressed in corporate-casual wear, Eddie Bauer from head to toe. His relaxed button-down shirt wasn't tight, but it fit well enough for me to see the definition of some of his muscles nestled beneath.

As soon as we sat down, I found myself staring at his angular jawline, which was lightly shadowed with stubble. The faint beard framed his face and led my eyes up to the closely cropped scalp on top of his head, which was slightly large for his body. My eyes lowered quickly, hoping he wouldn't notice me examining him, but I paused at his full lips, just as he stretched out his tongue and slid it across them.

He is a good-looking man, I thought. *Too bad he's so young.*

I glanced up and saw him looking back at me. Embarrassed, I dropped my head and began eating my lunch silently. I didn't look up until Catherine exclaimed, "Oh, it's already two fifteen. I've got to go. Is it cool if I leave you two here?"

"Go handle your business, girl. We'll be fine here," I said, waiting to see if Bryce would grimace at the thought of being alone with me. He didn't.

Once Catherine left, Bryce picked up his tray and took the seat directly in front of me. I was five foot ten, and my legs extended more than halfway across the underside of the cafeteria table, so when he sat down, our legs brushed up against one another.

"So, what's your deal?" asked Bryce, as he reached his hand under the table and firmly placed it on my thigh to stop it from bouncing up and down.

"What do you mean?" I asked. "Before you answer, can you take your hand off my leg?"

"My bad," Bryce replied. "I didn't mean anything by it. You were just shaking the whole table."

"Sorry, I didn't even realize I was doing that."

"Don't stress it. Now, to answer your question, I wanted to know why you've been checking me out."

"I was just looking at you. Don't read too much into it."

"Now you're acting shy. Okay, cool. Can I ask you a question, though?" he interrupted.

"Sure."

"Are you attracted to me? Because I'm attracted to you."

Stunned and unable to speak for a few seconds, I thought, *Who the hell asks someone that?* However, I didn't say that out loud.

"You are an attractive guy, but I don't date people I work with," I responded.

"Fair enough," he said.

After that day, Bryce and I exchanged only casual conversation at work—that is, until he cornered me at Jake's Dilemma and asked me if I wanted to go home with him.

My own arrogance got me into this mess, I thought, as the subway pulled into the Fiftieth Street station. *If I had just told him I've never had a one-night stand, I wouldn't be on this train, nervous as hell.*

I was silent, lost in my thoughts, until Bryce yelled and got my attention.

"You okay over there?" he shouted.

"Yes," I exclaimed, knowing that was the furthest thing from the truth.

He couldn't hear my response, though. The noise level had gotten so loud, I could barely hear myself.

As we barreled toward Forty-Second Street, my heart pounded in my chest like I was running a marathon. My anticipation level continued to rise as the train trucked into the station in question—the one that would determine if I'd break my dry spell or run home with my tail between my legs.

I glanced over at Bryce as the doors of the subway car opened and the motorman shouted, "Times Square."

Hordes of people filed out past me as I flip-flopped between going and not. Bryce just stood quietly, staring at me so deeply I was certain he was trying to read my mind. I glared back at him for a few moments, then mouthed, "What do you want me to do?"

"Whatever you want," he responded, with no discernible expression on his face.

Just then, I heard the motorman announce, "Stand clear of the closing doors"; that was followed by three short bells signaling that the car doors were going to shut.

"Guess you're coming, huh?" he yelled, just as I stepped back out of the path of the doors and watched them shut in front of my face.

What have I done? I wondered. *I don't even really know this man. He could be a serial killer or something. I'd better let someone know where I'm going, just in case.*

I'd talked a good game convincing Bryce I was self-assured and sexually free. In reality, I'd had very few sexual relationships. I was a serial monogamist. I went from one long-term relationship to another all of my adult life. I'd never even considered a one-night stand until Bryce mentioned it, but here I was, about to have one.

What are his expectations about me? I wondered. *I hope I can live up to them.*

Within seconds, we arrived at the Thirty-Fourth Street stop. Bryce extended his hand to me and said, "Are you ready?"

I should've said, "Hell no." Instead, a sense of calm washed over me and I said coyly, "Sure, why not?"

Bryce just smiled and guided me over to the walkway to the New Jersey PATH train, the next leg of our journey.

Unlike on the New York City subway, Bryce and I sat next to each other, in adjoining seats, on the PATH train.

"You okay?" Bryce asked, noticing I was twisting a knot in a small section of hair at the base of my neck.

"Why wouldn't I be?" I snapped.

"You just seemed like you were waffling back there."

"I was just wondering if you were worth my staying out all night," I said mockingly. "I do have to call my parents, though, to let them know I won't be back tonight."

"You still live with them?"

"Yeah," I said defensively. "I moved in with my folks a few months ago and trust me, it was quite an adjustment. I really hadn't lived with them since I was 14 and left for boarding school."

"So, I'm out with the real-life Tootie from The Fact of Life?" Bryce joked.

"Ha, ha," I chuckled. "I did live away at school but that's where the similarities end. Afterwards, I went to Boston College and then I stayed in Boston with my former roommate Diane for a little over four years. She and I moved to New Jersey together. Recently, though she decided it was time for her to live alone. I didn't have much time to look for a place so I moved into my parents' home."

"Is it weird living with them after all this time?" Bryce asked.

"To tell you the truth, it's not as strange as I thought. It's actually kind of cool getting to know them adult to adult. I've discovered my mom and I can talk about anything and my father and I are too much alike in both good and bad ways. It's definitely been interesting spending time with them that isn't due to a holiday or a crisis. My parents have helped me weather a lot of ups and downs. They've always had my back."

"You sound comfortable there with them."

"Oh, please know it's just temporary arrangement while I look for a house to buy."

"You're buying a house by yourself?"

"Believe me, I didn't imagine it this way, but I promised myself I'd own a house by the time I was thirty. I have the money, so I figure I might as well go for it."

"Very interesting," said Bryce, while looking me up and down. "You're not what I expected at all."

"And what was that?"

"I can say I didn't think you'd come home with me," replied Bryce.

"Then why did you ask?"

"I figured I might as well take a shot. I had a fifty-fifty chance that you'd say yes."

"And the fact that I might've had a few drinks tonight didn't make you think your odds might be better?"

"No," he exclaimed. "Besides, I didn't see you drink anything at all except for a Coke. So you tell me— why are you here? You're not beer goggling."

"You're right, I'm not drunk. I don't drink at all," I replied.

I almost told him the medication I took prevented me from drinking any alcohol, but I figured it would weird him out and ruin the relaxed atmosphere between us. So I said, "I guess I need some excitement in my life."

"And I'm it?" Bryce asked.

"I hope so," I responded. "By the way, where are we going for our good time?"

"To Jersey City," Bryce replied. "We should be there in ten to fifteen minutes."

"Great. My old roommate, Diane, lives there."

"Oh yeah, where?"

"She's right off Congress Street."

"It's a small world; that's just a few blocks from me."

Whew, I thought. *That's a relief. At least I know someone nearby in case he turns out to be a nut. I'd better call her when I get to Jersey to let her know what's going on.*

Within fifteen minutes, Bryce and I arrived at our destination, the Grove Street PATH station.

"Do you need to call your folks to let them know where you are?" Bryce asked, as we headed toward the escalator.

"You know, I do need to make a quick call, but I'll do it when we get up onto the street," I responded.

The moment we left the station, I whipped out my cell phone. First, I called my folks to tell them I'd be spending the night out. I omitted the fact that it was with a man. Immediately after, I dialed Diane. She and I had lived together for about eight years after college, and although we'd gone our separate ways, we remained extremely close. She would know that if I was calling this late, I must need something, that it must be important, so she'd answer right away.

Diane didn't disappoint. She answered her cell phone on the third ring.

"Hey, Dee," I said. "How are you?"

"I'm fine, but what's going on with you?" she asked, clearly curious about why I was calling at that hour of the night.

"I'm in your neck of the woods."

"Why? Did your car break down or something?" Diane queried.

"No."

"Did you get sick or something and can't make it home?"

"No, no, nothing like that. I'm out here because of a guy from work."

"Wait, what? Are you telling me you went home with some guy you work with?"

"Yeah, girl. I was out at this bar with Cat and—"

"You were out at a bar?" Diane asked, interrupting me. "You never go out. What's gotten into you? Did you take too many of your pills or something?"

"I just decided I'd better enjoy my life while I can."

"Are you sure about this?"

"I am."

"Then go get yours. You haven't been laid in a while. Maybe it'll make you less cranky."

"Whatever," I responded in a snotty tone. "Can you just grab a piece of paper so I can give you Bryce's information in case he turns out to be a nut?"

"I see," Diane said, fumbling for a piece of paper so she could write down Bryce's name, address, phone number, and physical description.

"If I don't call you back by midnight, call the police and then my parents," I said.

"What if you're too busy to call?" Diane asked, with a mischievous tone in her voice.

"From your lips to God's ear," I replied. "Let me get off this phone, though. He's waiting for me. Just look out for my call."

"I got you. Just relax and have a good time."

"I'll try. Love you."

"Love you too."

Once I hung up, I quickened my step to catch up to Bryce. He had walked about half a block up and was just pacing.

I sure hope he didn't walk away because he heard any part of my conversation, I thought as I approached him.

"Sorry I was on the phone so long," I said, trying to gauge if he was annoyed with me.

"No worries," Bryce responded. "I did think you changed your mind for a minute, though, and were asking your girlfriend to save you."

"Nah, nothing like that," I replied. "If that was true, I'd have just made a run for it and hopped back on the train."

Bryce laughed loudly, then began walking close enough to me that we probably appeared from a distance to be holding hands. My stomach was doing flips, a cross between exhilaration and nausea, as I grazed his arm with my fingers. Just that touch was enough to stir my desire for him. I couldn't wait to find out if we had even more chemistry. Thankfully, I didn't have to. We reached the stoop of the two-family, wood-framed house he called home in just minutes.

Bryce rifled through his pocket, dug out a ring of keys that would have rivaled a janitor's, and unlocked the front door. It swung open widely, revealing a steep staircase leading straight up to his second-floor apartment.

After he pushed open the door to his unit, I paused just over the threshold to take in my surroundings. Hardwood floors extended throughout his apartment, and a collection of ethnic art by artists like Justin Bua and Ernest Watson lined the walls.

My legs shook a bit when I stepped further inside. Noticing my apprehension, Bryce sauntered over to me, put his arm around the small of my waist, and ushered me into his living room. His touch was inviting, thrilling, even, and from that moment on, I wasn't afraid. I was anxious to know what the rest of him felt like.

"You know, you can take your shoes off," Bryce said, planting himself so close to me on the sofa, I could feel the breath as it left his mouth.

"I'm fine," I muttered, even though I was clenching my jaw so tightly, my teeth were starting to hurt.

"Relax," Bryce said, as he bent over and slid his hand down my calf to my slender ankles. Then he lifted my foot out of my black kitten heel. He drifted over to the other leg without looking up and did the same thing again.

"Now, don't you feel better?" he asked with a sheepish smile on his face.

Yes, I do, I thought but didn't tell him. I just tucked my feet underneath me so I was sitting Indian-style and went back to watching TV.

"So now what?" I asked.

"Right now we are going to watch Conan O'Brien," he said, stretching his arms across me, gently grazing my breasts with his forearms, before picking up the remote and raising the volume on the TV.

As he pulled back, Bryce turned to me and laid his two supple lips on top of mine until his were fully covering mine, and tickled the roof of my mouth with his tongue. My knees began to quake with delight.

Now that's *a first kiss*, I thought as I looked at him, trying to see if he felt the same thing I did.

"You didn't mind, did you?" Bryce asked.

I responded by drawing him to me and kissing him. My newfound aggression seemed to excite Bryce, but he took back the lead. He dragged his fingertips from my earlobes to the back of my neck and then down to the end of my shoulder-length hair, sending a chill down my spine. My entire body became weak, and I slumped into his arms.

Bryce laid me down on the sofa and slid his body on top of mine. He used his fingertips to lift up the edge of my blouse and crept up to my belly button. He ran his fingers around the rim of it before continuing the trip up to my breasts. He cupped them, then flicked the nipples with his fingertip; it was stimulating. I wanted more of him, all of him. But he suddenly stopped, stood up, and walked out of the room.

Confused, I wondered if I had done something to turn him off.

Does he want me to follow him into his room? I wondered.

I'd barely finished my thought when Bryce appeared in the doorway, fully erect and wearing a condom. I gawked at his girth and length as he came toward me.

Is he going to fit? Is this going to hurt? I wondered as Bryce placed both hands around my waist and drew me closer to the edge of the futon. He then began to undress me. Naked in front of him, I was unable to hide how I was reacting to his touch.

Bryce looked me in the eyes and said, "Slide forward, Nika. Closer, a little closer—now breathe."

He slowly placed himself inside me, inch by inch. No one had ever gotten me so wet without one stroke. Once he was completely inside, I placed both of my arms around his strong back. His fullness inside me was unlike anything I had ever experienced. No one had ever touched the spot in me he reached. It was ecstasy. I was moaning and groaning uncontrollably, releasing any and every sound my body spawned. The only time I was silent was when he'd grab my chin and bring me close for a kiss.

My audible pleasure seemed to arouse him, because Bryce quickly flipped me over, placed me up on my knees, and entered me from behind. We rose and fell in sync. We had a rhythm I had never known before. It felt as if we had been designed for each other. It didn't take long before my legs began to shudder and I felt a rush of satisfaction oozing from me.

Bryce put his mouth next to my ear and said, "I will stop if you want me to."

"No, don't stop," I replied, as I continued to savor his every movement.

Bryce quickened his pace, thrusting so fast and so hard, I could hear our bodies thrashing against each other like waves in a storm hitting rocks in the ocean. His breathing became labored, and faint sounds of whimpering started coming from him as sweat began to drip down his chest. I could feel droplets of it bead against my back. Seconds later, he let out a large grunt and I could feel his warmth fill the tip of the condom inside me.

He eased back and freed himself from me, careful to hold on to the base of the condom. The second he was out, I could feel moisture pour out of me, flowing freely down my legs and onto his sofa. Feeling the liquid seeping underneath his knee, Bryce quickly turned on the light right behind us to see exactly what was going on.

"I think you got your friend," he said.

"I don't think so," I responded.

I considered telling him I wasn't like other women; I didn't have a regular period. In fact, if it came four times a year, that was good for me.

"Well, there's blood on the sofa," he snapped.

I looked down and saw the pool of blood he was referring to that had collected beneath us.

"I'm so sorry," I said. "I don't know what's going on."

"Well, let me get you a towel," he said, racing across the living room to grab one.

"I'm so sorry," I shouted again as I collected my clothes off the floor and scurried into the bathroom, passing right by him. "I will help you clean that up."

Mortified, I grabbed a washcloth off the sink and tried to wash up, but the blood wouldn't slow down. I grabbed wads of toilet paper off the roll and wrapped it around the seat of my underwear, thinking it would be enough to get me to Diane's house, where I could get a proper pad or tampon. However, the second I raised up off the toilet seat, more blood poured down my legs.

I can't believe this is happening, I thought. *Why can't I be normal for just one night? Why is this happening to me?*

Agitated, I began to frantically look for anything to stop the bleeding.

What am I supposed to do? I wondered, unable to find anything to help. *I'm trapped and there's nothing I can do.*

I began to shake as moments later when it hit me that this wasn't an ordinary period; it was something far worse. I'd suffered hemorrhages before, but I prayed, *Not now.*

"I hate to ask," I yelled through the partially open door, "but do you have sweatpants I can borrow?"

"Yeah, let me get you a pair," Bryce said. "Are you all right?"

"Um, actually, I don't think so," I answered. "I may need your help."

"What's going on?"

"I need you to grab my cell phone and dial my friend Diane. Tell her she needs to come get me right now."

"Oh, okay," he said, stuttering, clearly unnerved by my response.

I'm completely humiliated. He must think I'm some sort of freak. Great, I thought. *If that's not bad enough I'm bleeding to death and I have no way to get out of here. I wish I could just flush myself down this toilet to escape.*

I peeled off my bloody pants and laid them on the floor of his bathroom, next to the towel I'd snatched off the rack to place under my feet so I didn't dirty his white tiles. I then turned on the shower to rinse myself off while I waited for him to bring me the sweatpants and for Diane to arrive.

It was beginning to look like a crime scene in there: blood on the toilet paper roll, bloody clothes on the floor, and a pink residue lining the bathtub.

This is a nightmare, I thought. *I've got to clean this up.*

I bent over to wipe out the tub with a sponge, when I started to feel weak. I was getting more and more light-headed, and a tingling sensation was shooting up my legs.

"I just spoke to your friend," Bryce shouted. "I'm going to go meet her outside."

"Okay," I yelled, as I lowered myself back down onto the toilet seat. "Do you have those pants?"

"Yeah. Can I open the door?" he asked.

"You're going to have to, because I can't get there," I responded.

Bryce's face turned gray instantly after he opened the bathroom door and saw the carnage inside.

"Oh my God," he whispered to himself. "If I get out of this and she doesn't die, I will never have sex again."

He doesn't think I can hear him, I thought. *If only he knew I feel the same exact way.*

Bryce didn't say anything to me. He just handed me the sweatpants and closed the door behind him.

Tears began to run down my face as I thought, *I've got to get out of this guy's house. My God, my God, I can't believe this. Please don't let me die here.* I repeated the same thing at least twenty-five times, before I heard a faint knock at the door.

"Yes," I shouted.

"It's me, Diane. Can I come in?"

"Yes, please, please, please get me out of here," I begged, sobbing uncontrollably.

"Calm down," Diane said. "We're going to go, but first we have to get you dressed."

Diane took the blood-filled rag over to the sink and rinsed it out. She came back and wiped down my legs as best she could before helping me shimmy into his sweatpants. The blood was still leaking out of me so fast that those pants were stained in seconds too.

"We have to take you to the hospital," Diane said.

Diane placed her arms around me and helped guide me out into his foyer. She leaned me up against the wall, then summoned Bryce for help.

"I need to get her to the hospital, and I need your help," she said.

"Okay, let me throw on some shoes," he replied. "In the meantime, why don't you run down and hail a cab, and I'll get her down the stairs?"

Bryce threw his arm around my waist and gently walked me over to the top of the stairs. He looked down at them and must've decided I wouldn't be able to descend them in my condition, because he scooped me up and carried me down that flight of stairs. When we got to the bottom, he asked, "Can you stand?"

"Yes," I replied.

"Stand here while I see where Diane is with the cab."

Bryce shuffled out the door, returning less than two minutes later with Diane. Each of them took a side and ushered me out the door and into the cab.

"Saint Mary's Hospital," Diane yelled as the cab sped away from the curb.

It cost $15 to go the twelve blocks from Bryce's house to the hospital, but no one quibbled about the price.

"I'll pay it," Bryce said. "Just get her inside."

Diane and I struggled into the emergency room, where a nurse met us almost instantly. Diane explained to her that I was having a massive hemorrhage, had lost a lot of blood, and was in need of urgent care. As a nurse, Diane knew exactly what to say to get me the help I needed. She always spoke for me whenever she took me to the hospital.

I didn't sit in the waiting room or fill out paperwork; I was rushed into the back. Diane aided the nurses in removing my clothes, getting me into a gown, and helping me lie down on the gurney so I could be wheeled into a room for treatment. I had been lying there for only a few minutes before the nurse noticed blood running out from underneath me.

"Lift up," the nurse said. "You need to sit on top of this stack of towels until the doctor comes in. We'll also get you started on an IV."

I didn't even feel the stick of the needle when she started the IV line, because by then even my arms were numb from blood loss. I was drifting in and out of consciousness, and I was freezing. The nurse dumped as many as five blankets on top of me to try to keep me warm, but nothing worked.

Diane noticed I seemed to be in greater distress, so she rushed over to the nurses' station and said, "You hung a regular IV. She's been losing blood. She should've had one with lactated Ringer's solution. Please get me a doctor now. She's bleeding out."

The next thing I remember is the doctor asking me if I could be pregnant.

"No," I said, fainting, thinking to myself, *Before tonight I hadn't even had sex in nearly two years.*

"If you can hear me, you are hemorrhaging, so we need to perform a DNC to stop the bleeding; that's when we dilate the cervix and scrape and vacuum out the uterus."

What? I thought. *Just do whatever you need to do in order to save me.*

"You need to sign the consent form," the doctor continued.

Are you fucking kidding me? I thought.

I scribbled my name as best I could, and then it was lights out. I remember nothing until I woke up in a recovery room, sore and dazed.

"Ms. Beamon, are you awake?" the doctor, who didn't bother to tell me his name, asked. "How are you feeling?"

"Okay," I mumbled.

"The procedure went well. You will still have a little bleeding for the next few days, but we will give you a prescription for birth control pills to regulate your hormones. Five days from now, you should follow up with your primary care physician."

"Okay," I said, slurring the word.

"Did your doctor tell you before that you have a condition called PCOS or polycystic ovary syndrome?" Not waiting for a response, he continued to explain, "Well, you ruptured several large hemorrhagic cysts, and that's what caused your bleeding."

"Okay," I said, slurring again.

"Get some rest, and I will check on you in a few hours. We will do an ultrasound then to make sure we got everything."

I drifted back into a deep sleep, awakening to the sound of a male voice in my ear.

"Are you okay?" Bryce whispered.

My eyelids fluttered as I struggled to open them to see who was speaking. To my surprise, Bryce was standing there. Just over his shoulder, I could see the clock. It read 4:00 AM.

"I'm okay," I said at a barely audible level.

"I had to see for myself that you were all right," he continued. "I won't keep you. I just wanted to check on you."

"Thank you. Thank you for everything," I said as a tear trickled down my cheek.

"No worries at all," he replied. "I'm just glad you are going to be okay; that's the most important thing."

"Don't you have to be to work at seven AM?" I asked.

"I do, but I couldn't leave until I checked on you," he answered. "I'll be fine. I'm a warrior."

Bryce pushed my bangs off my face, then placed a tender kiss in the center of my forehead.

"Get some rest," he said as he turned and walked out the room. "I'll talk to you later."

Yeah, right, I thought. *He'll talk to me in the office, but I'd bet that's about it.*

I couldn't get the distressing thought that I'd scared Bryce off out of my mind until I passed out. I slept until nearly 10:00 AM the next day; then I felt my bed moving.

"Where am I going?" I asked the man pushing me down a long corridor.

"I'm taking you to radiology so you can get an internal ultrasound."

"Oh," I replied.

The orderly parked my gurney right under the RADIOLOGY sign while I waited for a room. It didn't take long before I was in a private room, meeting the second doctor of my hospital visit.

"I'm Dr. Rabine, and I'll be doing your internal ultrasound. I'm going to place some jelly on your belly. It's going to be a bit cold. Afterward I'm going to place this instrument inside you and take some pictures," she said.

If I hadn't known better, it would have appeared as if she were planning to insert a giant vibrator or one of those neck massagers inside me. But it looked harmless enough, so I wasn't concerned at all as I watched her wrap the head of the device in plastic to prepare it for insertion.

Dr. Rabine pressed down on my stomach and began sliding the instrument inside me. I felt a burning sensation followed by excruciating pain, as if a razor blade were being dragged across my insides. I could barely remain still on the table as she continued to slam the wand up against the walls of my uterus, snapping image after image, which appeared on a tiny screen on the machine in front of me. Teardrops ran from my eyes as I squirmed and began crawling up the gurney, trying to extricate myself from the device.

"I'm almost done," Dr. Rabine said in the most reassuring tone she could muster.

"I can't," I hollered. "I can't take it. Please stop."

"We're just about done," she replied, stroking my hand, trying to comfort me. "That's it. You can relax now."

Dr. Rabine stayed by me even as I rolled onto my side and wept while waiting for the orderly to come back. By the time he arrived, I was composed and ready to go.

My parents were waiting in my room with smiles plastered on their faces when I got there. Diane had called them and filled them in about what was going on with me. She later told me they had asked, "How serious is it? Is she going to make it?"

Diane said she answered, "She's a fighter. She's survived worse. She'll be fine."

"How are you, baby girl?" my mother asked, looking me over to see if anything was visibly wrong. She was so in tune with me she could always tell how I was feeling, and sometimes what I was thinking, just by looking at me.

It was the same question she asked every time she and my dad came to pick me up from a hospital.

"You know me," I replied. "I'm hanging in there."

"I brought this for you, baby," my father said, taking off his cowboy hat and sitting it on the table in front of me. He then handed me a pig wearing a golf outfit. "You can focus on this whenever you are in pain."

My father started giving me mini sculptures of pigs after my trip to the hospital several years earlier. He selected pigs because they were my favorite animal and sure to make me smile. I also supposed the figurines were his way of reminding me that he was watching over me even when he physically couldn't d so. By the time he handed me the newest one, my collection was at 20.

"Thanks, Daddy," I replied, choking up. "I'll add him to the group."

"Dad and I talked to the doctor, and he says you're going to be okay," my mother said, with a sense of relief in her voice.

Yeah, until the next time, I thought.

"You can leave tomorrow. Daddy will come back to pick you up and take you home," said my mom as she pulled my blanket up and tucked me in.

I didn't know what to say. I just wondered, *Will my parents spend the rest of their lives taking care of me? Shouldn't this be the other way around?*

Chapter 2: Exorcist Baby

Bryce's Bose Wave radio went off at 5:45 AM sharp, signaling it was time for him to get ready to go to work. I'd usually reach over him to hit snooze so he could get fifteen more minutes of sleep. When he woke up, I'd watch him stroll toward the shower and I'd fall back to sleep. But that hadn't happened in the last six months. I'd barely been able to wake myself up, with or without an alarm. Bryce rolled with the punches, never complaining about the change in routine, just like he'd been doing since the first night we were together. Clearly, my near-death experience hadn't scared him off, because he called me two days later to ask me out on our first official date.

"How are you doing?" Bryce asked in a soft voice. "Are you feeling better?"

"I am," I responded. "Thanks for asking. Sorry I didn't call you back sooner. My dad told me someone called the day I got home from the hospital, but he couldn't make out the name. I didn't know it was you until I went downstairs and checked the answering machine."

"It's not a problem," Bryce replied. "I figured you were recuperating."

"Well, I should let you go," I said, fearing he had called me only out of guilt.

"Wait a second," he said firmly. "I was wondering if you wanted to go out and get something to eat sometime, when you are better, of course."

"Uh, yes," I said, stunned he had even considered asking me out.

"You sound surprised," Bryce said. "Why?"

"Do you have to ask?" I replied. "The last time I saw you, I ruined your sofa, your bathroom floor, and a pair of your sweatpants. Oh, and I almost died."

"True," Bryce chuckled. "But I liked you up to that point. Besides, shit happens."

Is he for real? I wondered. *No one is this understanding.*

"If that's really how you feel, I'd like a do-over," I said.

"Easy, killer," Bryce quipped. "I'm talking about taking it nice and slow this time."

"Sounds good," I responded.

Two Saturdays after that call, Bryce and I went on our first official date; a second and a third quickly followed. In a month's time, we were spending at least three nights a week together. And by the time I learned to shut off his alarm clock, two **years** later, Bryce and I practically lived together.

So, that morning started the same as dozens before. I rose to shut off the bullhorn noise coming from Bryce's alarm clock, but the motion of lifting my torso off the bed triggered a Linda Blair in *The Exorcist*–like response. Instead of pea soup flying out of my mouth, blood spewed from my throat and landed in a puddle on the ivory carpet below. The splash hit the ground and left small dots of blood all over the mirrored closet, the dresser, the bed ruffle, and Bryce's slippers.

The sound of retching must've been really loud, because it woke Bryce from his sleep. Without opening his eyes, he muttered, "What's going on, Nika? You okay?"

I tried to answer him, but before I could utter a word, throw-up mixed with stomach acid burned up my esophagus and flew from my mouth, muffling my words. I slid off the edge of the bed and down to the floor.

Maybe I can crawl to the bathroom, I thought. However, a stabbing pain in my gut prevented me from moving.

Bryce wiped his eyes and reached for his glasses, without which he couldn't see his hand in front of his face.

"Oh, shit," Bryce shouted, seeing blood saturating the carpet. "I'll get a bucket."

I tried to stop the torrent of fluid pouring out of me by shutting my mouth tightly and putting my hand over it, but all that did was cause me to gag and make it hard for me to breathe. So I let go and watched, helplessly, as the deluge landed on the carpet while I ran toward the bathroom.

Bryce rushed past me, back into the room, armed with latex gloves, a bucket filled with Comet and water, and a giant sponge. He propped himself up on his forearms and used his full weight to scrub the stain out.

I was kneeling in front of the porcelain god, purging every ounce of fluid in me. In between dry heaves, I sipped a palmful of water to try to calm my angry stomach down. Oddly, the water seemed to only make matters worse, so I just leaned there until I thought the worst had passed. After about ten minutes, I walked out of the bathroom fully collected and with Scope-smelling breath.

"What's wrong?" Bryce asked repeatedly, as he continued to scrub as hard as he could, finally restoring the light color to his carpet. "We need to get you to the hospital."

"I'll be fine," I said as I hobbled over to the bed, out of his way. "Let me just rest for a second, and then I'll help you clean this up."

"You sure you're okay?" he asked. "Vomiting blood isn't normal."

"I know," I quipped. "Since when have I been considered normal?"

"Stop screwing around," he said, not even cracking a smile. "Look around. You must've ruptured something—maybe one of your cysts again. We're going to either the hospital or Dr. Thomas."

Two sick calls later, Bryce and I made the drive from Jersey City through the Holland Tunnel and into Manhattan to see Dr. Thomas, the primary care physician we shared. We got a space in front of his Sixty-Eighth Street office in a matter of minutes, but that was the last thing that happened quickly. Without an appointment, we sat in the waiting area for nearly an hour and a half. Then I sat in exam room five alone for another fifteen minutes, before Janet, the nurse-practitioner, took my blood pressure, height, weight, and temperature, which was hovering around 101—not unusual for me.

"So, what seems to be the matter today?" Dr. Thomas asked as he strolled into the room, carrying his laptop containing my gigantic medical file, which he used to need an entire arm to carry.

"Well, I threw up blood again this morning. It seems to be happening more frequently. Does this have anything to do with my PCOS?"

"No, between five and eighteen percent of women have that condition. Other than infrequent periods, excessive hair growth, and an increased risk of type two diabetes, PCOS really doesn't pose a serious problem. It sounds like something else is going on with you. I think you need to see a gastroenterologist. He'll take a look at your stomach, esophagus, and intestines; that may give us a better idea of the problem."

"Okay. When can I go?"

"Today," he replied, furiously striking the keys on his computer. "I'm going to have Janet call Dr. Raymond to see if he can take you at Roosevelt Hospital right now."

Dr. Thomas picked up his computer and walked out of the room without making eye contact with me. If he had, he'd have seen my hands begin to shake with nervousness.

"Here's your referral slip," Dr. Thomas said. "Just take this to Dr. Raymond's office, and he'll fit you right in."

I'm sure this means another hour-and-a-half wait, I thought.

I hopped down from the exam table with my referral slip in hand, collecting myself before going out to the waiting room to give Bryce the update.

Bryce didn't bat an eye; he just said, "Let's go."

We meandered side by side, making very little conversation, ten blocks and three avenues over to Dr. Raymond's office in the medical building connected to the hospital. I wondered why Bryce hadn't asked what Dr. Thomas had said or what this new doctor was supposed to do for me, but I didn't mention it. I figured we'd have plenty of time to kill in Dr. Raymond's waiting room, so I'd question Bryce then.

Surprisingly, my butt had barely touched one of the hard, cold plastic chairs in the lobby of Dr. Raymond's office when his nurse called me into the back.

"You want me to come with you?" Bryce asked, with the first bit of trepidation I'd heard in his voice all day.

"No, I'm good," I responded, even though that was a complete lie. I had no idea what the doctor might find, and the possibilities frightened me. But there was no time to express my fears to Bryce anyway; I was whisked into an exam room, where Dr. Raymond was waiting.

"Come in," Dr. Raymond said, with his back to me. "Dr. Thomas tells me you have been having some stomach issues. Tell me about that."

I began to ramble uncontrollably. I told him about every meal I ate and how none of them agreed with me or caused me to puke up blood. I wasn't sure what he needed to know or not know. I just figured I'd cover my bases, especially since I'd never been to a gastroenterologist before.

Dr. Raymond didn't stop me from babbling. He feverishly scribbled on a chart on the desk in front of him. When he finally stopped writing and I got my tongue to stop wagging, he said, "I think the best thing for us to do at this point is to schedule an endoscopy."

"A what?" I asked.

"Here is a pamphlet that will tell you about the procedure, but basically, I will give you mild anesthesia, then snake this flexible tube down your esophagus and take a look at what's going on. If I find anything unusual, like a cyst, I can use a tool built into the tube and take it out right then," Dr. Raymond said.

"Okay, how soon should I do that?"

"As soon as possible," he replied.

I was still reeling from this news when Dr. Raymond asked, "Have you noticed any blood in your stool?"

I wanted to say that I didn't make it a habit of looking in the toilet after I go, but I responded, "I don't know."

"You think you could get me a sample right now?" Dr. Raymond asked.

I was screaming, *What the fuck?* in my head, but, again, what could I say besides "I guess so"?

I grabbed the small cup he gave me and headed off to the bathroom to do the most humiliating thing I'd ever done: shit in a cup and hand it over to someone else with a smile on my face.

I tried to hide the cup under my arm as I walked down the hall from the bathroom, passing two other rooms with people in them. When I got back to my room, I slunk inside and handed the cup to the doctor. He unscrewed the cap and wiped a piece of paper through the feces. He then lifted it to his face and said, "I think you need a colonoscopy too. Your stool shows the presence of blood."

Does that mean I have colon cancer? I wondered. I didn't ask, because I knew I wasn't prepared to handle the answer, so I just said, "Is a colonoscopy a lot like the endoscopy?"

"We do use a scope similar to the one I showed you, but, of course, you know it goes in the other end. My nurse will have to give you a prescription for the solution you'll need to drink to clean you out so we can see what's going on. It comes with flavor packets to make it more palatable."

I highly doubt something that is going to make me shit until I'm clean as a whistle could taste good, I thought, but I didn't want to burst his bubble, so I just asked, "Can I schedule both on the same day?"

"No, let's do the endoscopy first; then we will do the colonoscopy a day or so later. You will need someone to drive you home both days, because of the anesthesia."

I gathered my pamphlets and what was left of my dignity and left the room. I walked out to the front desk, arranged my appointment dates, and collected Bryce for the journey back to his apartment.

The week between the day I left Dr. Raymond's office and the endoscopy date passed without Bryce's and my talking about it. I tried not to think about it and immersed myself in work, which consisted mostly of writing and editing stories about the misery, missteps, and misfortune of others, then airing it on TV. Doing four newscasts a day, I barely had time to pee, let alone any minutes to spare obsessing about someone peering inside me to determine what was making me fall apart.

Every once in a while the what-ifs would sneak in: *What if he finds something serious, like cancer; what if his poking around makes things worse; what if he can't figure out what's wrong with me; what if I have to take even more drugs?* I was already taking Provera for my hemorrhages, metformin twice a day for my insulin resistance syndrome, and Tums like Tic Tacs to ease my never-ending heartburn.

I got up the Wednesday of my exam with nothing on my mind; my what-ifs had finally quieted. I knew, if nothing else, I would finally have answers to the questions that had nagged me. Instead, my biggest concern was over what to wear. I figured I should be in an outfit that was easy to get on and off. I couldn't get that stupid thing my mother used to tell me out of my head: *make sure you have clean, nice underwear on.* So I pulled out my best Victoria's Secret bikini-cut gray briefs and matching semipadded bra and threw them on underneath my gray-and-pink Reebok track suit. The outfit had an added benefit: it had enough pockets for me to stuff my phone, keys, and wallet into, without needing a pocketbook.

Dressed and raring to go, I climbed into the passenger seat of my Nissan Maxima—a side of the car I hadn't ridden on often, and one that reminded me how fragile I'd become, because I couldn't even cart myself around. That was all I need to set me on edge again.

I couldn't stop myself from commenting on Bryce's driving skills.

"You're slamming on the brakes too hard!" I shouted.

At the next intersection, I exclaimed, "Are you trying to kill me before we get there? If not, slow down."

I fully expected Bryce to yell for me to shut up or snap back, but he didn't, not even once. He kept his unusually mellow demeanor the entire way until we walked into the doctor's office.

"I'll be here when you get out, Nika," he said, giving me a long embrace.

"Ms. Beamon," the nurse said, interrupting us.

"Yes, that's me," I responded.

I waited for the nurse to say something else or at least acknowledge that I had responded. Rather, she simply pointed to the exam room on the left, right past the door, and began to walk away.

I reluctantly made my way over there and plopped myself down on the exam-room table.

"Take off everything except for your underwear. The anesthesiologist will be in to talk to you soon," shouted the nurse as she shuffled past my room on her way to God only knew where.

Why do I have to be naked if he's just going to look down my throat? I wondered. *How am I supposed to relax for this exam knowing I'm in a room full of strangers, naked, with my double Ds flopping around underneath this flimsy gown?*

I remained on edge until the anesthesiologist, who said his name so fast I couldn't understand it, burst into the room.

He sped through a host of questions—What's your name? What's your birth date? Do you have any allergies?—before he started explaining what he was going to do to me. He said he was going to put a port into a vein in my hand and connect an IV line. Then I was expected to sit with this foreign object attached to me until I was called into an exam room.

Once there, I'd be laid on my side with something stuck between my teeth to keep my mouth open, and he'd finally administer a drug that would likely knock me out. The aim of all his droning on was to get me to sign a series of forms granting him and the doctor immunity from any damages should I die or suffer any injury.

While he's got these forms to protect him, I thought, *who is protecting me?*

I stared at the paperwork, debating whether I had the option not to sign it. I didn't feel like I did, especially after the anesthesiologist and nurse kept pestering me about it. So I shelved my reservations and signed his forms.

As soon as the deed was done, the anesthesiologist jammed a needle into my hand and covered it with a rectangular piece of tape to keep it in place. Afterward, he stood up and left the room without even asking me if I was in any pain, which I was.

Chilly and anxious, I sat in the exam room for at least ten more minutes alone before the nurse came in and instructed me to follow her. She didn't ask how I was doing or if I had any fears, questions, anything. Hell, she didn't even look back to make sure I was following her. The only time she checked to ensure I was even there was when we got to the procedure room.

"Climb onto the bed and lie with your head on the pillow," she barked. "Make sure you are on your left side, then open your mouth."

As soon as I followed her commands, the nurse stuck a plastic piece into my mouth; it had a hole in the center that the camera could be threaded through. I felt like a pig at a luau.

"Let me have your hand," she squawked.

I stuck my arm forward, and the nurse connected my IV line to what appeared to be a plain bag of saline.

She didn't tell me what the cool fluid coursing through my veins was, and I didn't want to ask, because I feared her icy manner would cause her to make some callous statement I wasn't in the mood to hear.

When the nurse stepped away, I tried to reach the bag, swinging my arm wildly to get the words in a readable position without lifting my head off the pillow. I quickly realized this was a futile endeavor and just lay there, letting whatever the clear solution was run through me. Just as I got up the nerve to try again, the anesthesiologist came in with a large needle filled with another clear solution.

"This isn't going to hurt," he said, "but you might feel a slight burning sensation."

The anesthesiologist lifted my hand, stuck the needle into the port, and injected the drug into me. I felt nothing, at least not right away.

Dr. Raymond entered the room, fully dressed in scrubs, just as my head was starting to feel fuzzy. My eyelids felt heavy, like someone was physically trying to shut them. I could see only snapshots of him as he walked toward me. "How are you feeling?" Dr. Raymond asked. "Are you sleepy yet?"

"A little," I muttered.

"In a few minutes, we are going to start the exam. I'm going to insert this tube into your mouth, so I need you to remain still and swallow hard for me three times. Okay?"

I did just that, feeling the gentle scraping of the flexible tubing going down my esophagus. I initially felt like I was gagging or going to throw up, but once I relaxed it went straight down. Moments later, I passed out. I didn't wake up until twenty minutes later. I knew time had elapsed only when I looked at the monitor beside me.

"Ms. Beamon, how are you feeling?" Dr. Raymond asked.

I parted my crusty lips and replied, "I'm fine."

"We are going to take you to the recovery room now. Watch your step," he said as he helped me swing my legs off the side of the bed in the procedure room and stumble onto the floor. I staggered into the adjoining room, flopped down on the bed in there, and went back to sleep. I have no
idea how long I was out that time, but I awoke to the same question from Dr. Raymond: "How are you feeling, Ms. Beamon?" I almost thought it was a bad case of déjà vu, until I opened one eye, looked at my surroundings, and noticed I was indeed in the recovery room.

"Ms. Beamon," he repeated, "are you awake? Can you hear me?"

"I think so," I answered as I struggled to sit up.

"Your exam went well, but we did find a few problems."

I shook off some of my grogginess so I could pay better attention to what he was saying.

"You have a hiatal hernia, esophagus dysplasia, and a few cysts, which I have removed. I've also taken some biopsies. I will have the results in a few days."

"What does all of this mean?" I asked.

"Well, it looks like you've got a very severe case of GERD, or gastroesophageal reflux disease. I'm not sure yet if it's a condition called Barrett's esophagus."

"Is this why I've been throwing up blood?"

"It might be," Dr. Raymond responded.

"Could all the drugs I've taken over the years have caused this problem?" I asked.

"It's hard to say what's caused the damage," Dr. Raymond answered. "It's just important that we correct it."

"So, how do you fix it?"

"I'm going to prescribe a few drugs to help with your discomfort. I'll give you some diet tips and tips on how to sleep to keep the acid down. If those don't work, we will have to talk about surgery."

"Surgery?" I said anxiously. "What kind?"

"There are a few options, but in your case I'd suggest laparoscopic Nissen fundoplication. I will explain it to you if the drugs don't work. For now, just try the drugs and see how they go." When he finished speaking, Dr. Raymond got up and exited the room

I assume this surgery is serious, since he doesn't want to give me details, I thought.

The additional drugs, the prospect of surgery, and the knowledge that I had to wait for my biopsy results were swimming in my head. I hadn't sorted out how I felt about any of it by the time he came back, waving four prescriptions.

"Here is a prescription for Protonix, for your erosive esophagitis and excess stomach acid; Reglan, an antinausea medication; omeprazole, a proton pump inhibitor; and nortriptyline, an antidepressant also used for pain relief. These drugs may make you drowsy, but you should adjust. I will see you in two days for your colonoscopy."

Chapter 3: Which End Is Up?

I couldn't drink any more of the mucus-like liquid without gagging. My stomach was full, my tongue was coated with slime, and my bladder felt like it would leak if I took a step. Yet those symptoms were nothing compared with the percolating going on down below.

Nothing I have been through could make me more unattractive than I am right now, I thought, as I raced to the bathroom in Bryce's apartment.

I had barely sat down on the toilet seat when the floodgates opened. The squirting and farting noises were so loud, they drowned out the bathroom fan and most certainly could be heard in the living room, where Bryce was sitting, even though he had the TV blaring.

I flushed every few minutes, hoping that would cut down on the stench coming from the bathroom. Time seemed to drag on in there. I'd read so many magazines, I couldn't read another. I started keeping track of the time by cracking the bathroom door so I could listen to the different sitcoms end and come on.

It took nearly two hours for me to finally finish up. By then wiping myself felt like I was dragging a Brillo pad across my rump. It hurt so badly that I had to wait a while before I could pull up my panties.

I washed my hands like a surgeon preparing for an operation, rinsing and repeating so many times, my palms turned bright pink. Embarrassed, I cracked the door open slightly, hoping the Lysol I had sprayed would kill some of the stench so it would be almost bearable in there in case Bryce had to go.

Bryce didn't seem to notice or care about the smell as he walked up to the door and said, "You okay in there? I heard the water, so I thought you were done."

"I'm fine," I replied. "Clean as a whistle."

"I'll bet," Bryce chuckled. "Come out and sit with me."

"I'll come out, but I think I've been sitting long enough," I responded, finally laughing about the situation.

Bryce and I snuggled on the sofa together for the next hour, quietly watching our favorite drama before heading to bed.

We were more affectionate that night than we had been in a while. I hadn't felt much like cozying up to him after I'd found a text message he had sent to another woman, telling her he loved her. I came across it innocently enough a few weeks prior. I was in his bathroom sitting on the toilet when I noticed, what I thought was my phone, on one of the built in shelves in front of me. Perplexed, I picked it up. Part of me knew it wasn't my cell because I generally didn't bring it into the bathroom with me. However, I wasn't completely sure because the plethora of drugs I was on frequently left me feeling disoriented. Of course, part of the confusion stemmed from the fact that Bryce and I had the same phone.

I was aware the moment I picked the cell up and flipped it open that it was Bryce's. Still, I couldn't put it down. Curiosity got the better of me. So, I scrolled through his messages, viewing his many message professing his love and happiness with the other woman. As had begun a regular occurrence, I confronted Bryce with what I found the moment I flew out of the battle. For once, I didn't cry. I think I'd become numb.

Bryce gave me his same old lines: "I wake up next to you nearly every day. You're the one I take home to meet my family. I haven't been with anyone as long as you." When he realized that was doing very little to stem

the fury mounting within me he went to the words that never failed him: "I take you to the doctor, care for and clean up after you. I do that
because I love you. You are my best friend. I can't imagine my life without you. The other woman means nothing to me." I immediately melted. I hoped he was telling the truth. I needed to believe he was because I wasn't certain how I could cope with my never-ending bouts with illness without his emotional and physical support.

Bryce's infidelity was nothing new, though. Our first year together, I found a phone number from a woman he'd met in Washington, DC, while interning. They'd met up again in New York, and he'd begun seeing her at the same time he was seeing me. A few months into his affair with her, Bryce made a proclamation: "I think we're too different. I've met someone whom I have more in common with, and I think I'm going to stay with her." A month later, he changed his mind.

Six months after I reconciled with Bryce, I thought things were going well, until I stayed home sick at his apartment one day. I was helping him complete an article for work on his computer, when an instant message popped up from another woman. I knew I shouldn't even read it, but I was overcome with curiosity. I just replied with a simple hello. She said, "Hey, baby." My stomach sank, because I knew in that instant Bryce had a relationship with that woman. Then intuition told me she wasn't the only one.

I opened his email account, uncovering a treasure trove of correspondence with even more women, most of it inappropriate for a man who was supposed to be dating me. Infuriated, I picked up Bryce's house phone and called him at work.

"Bryce, tell me something," I shouted without even saying hello.

"Uh-oh," Bryce replied. "What did I do now?"

"Are you cheating on me?" I asked.

"No," he quickly replied.

"Don't lie to me," I yelled. "I'm sitting at your computer, and your messages would indicate otherwise."

"You opened my messages?" Bryce asked with bass in his voice.

"Just tell me the truth."

Bryce hung up, refusing to come clean about what he'd been doing.

He thinks he can hang up on me and that's the end of this, I thought. *Not even close. Either he will answer to me or I will get the answers I need from all of his women.*

I composed an email to all the women I could find in his email inbox, making sure everyone could see each other's email address, including Bryce's at work. When I was finished, I called Bryce back and gave him a choice to make.

"Tell me the truth, or I will email all of your women," I snapped.

"Do what you have to do," Bryce said with annoyance in his voice.

"Okay, then," I said as I hit the send button on his computer. Within moments, replies came in.

Bryce immediately called me back and shouted, "I can't believe you did that."

"I asked you to be honest with me, and you wouldn't, so I needed to find out what was going on behind my back," I replied.

"You had no right!" Bryce screamed.

"I had every right. I take pills every day to stop my own body from killing me. You think I am just going to let you do it? You are sleeping with God knows who, protected or not, risking my life."

"I trust you enough to leave you in my house, and this **is** what you do?"

"What *I* do?" I exclaimed. "What about what *you've* been doing?"

"It still doesn't give you the right to go through my stuff and violate my privacy."

"Stop changing the subject," I said, crying hysterically. "Tell me why! Why did you do this? Am I not enough? Is it because I'm sick and I fall asleep at nine o'clock? Is it because I can't go out drinking with you and don't have the energy for clubbing?"

"No," Bryce replied.

"Then why? Why would you hurt me like this?"

"I'm sorry I hurt you, but it still doesn't give you the right to snoop."

"Maybe you're right, but why couldn't you just tell me you didn't want me anymore?"

"Because that would be a lie," he answered. "I want you. I just fucked up. I wanted it all, you and them. That's the truth."

"You think I don't hate not having the energy to run around with you, have a good time, or make love to you whenever I want?" I asked.

"I know, Nika," Bryce said in his reassuring voice. "Calm down."

"How can I?"

"Look, I should've told you I was seeing other women. I just didn't want to lose you."

"You can always be honest with me."

"I will try from now on."

I blocked out Bryce's affairs with other women, and our relationship flourished for another year, until I caught him with his hand in the cookie jar again. Growing weary, I thought of breaking up with him, but he'd become my best friend. He was the person I talked to about my hopes and fears. He held my hand when I was at my weakest points becoming my greatest support besides my parents. He was the man who made me laugh instead of crying and with whom I spent the vast majority of my free time. He was attentive to my every need and never put anyone else before me. So I stayed. Two years later, I was still clinging to the man who'd repeatedly helped save me in so many ways. However, Bryce and I weren't as affectionate as we had been before I'd found out about his chronic cheating. Our emotional connection had replaced a physical one. I often used my illness to avoid being intimate with him, especially after I hadn't seen him for days. I couldn't shake the thought that when he wasn't with me, he was probably with other women. It disgusted me and made me feel completely disinterested in having sex with someone who could share

himself so easily with someone else. I couldn't. Even worse, I regularly felt as if I didn't have the physical allure to keep his attention. After all, I didn't curl or blow out my hair, opting instead to wear my hair in a ponytail with a tight bun. Putting on makeup wasn't something I concerned myself with either. And my clothes were simple and picked for comfort rather than fashion. An outfit merely had to be easy to get on and off for doctor's appointments.

Yet the night before I was to go in for my colonoscopy, I didn't think about our sordid past. I just looked at the man who'd held my hand at so many doctors' appointments, and I was overcome with love. I needed to

feel love, especially on the eve of getting even more bad medical news, so I rolled over onto Bryce's side of the bed, climbed on top of him, and initiated a marathon lovemaking session.

I was exhausted, in a good way, when I awoke to head to Dr. Raymond's surgical suite at the hospital the next morning for the colonoscopy. I arrived on time for the exam, even though being punctual isn't my strong suit. I figured the quicker I got there, the sooner I could stop obsessing about what it would be like.

I shuffled into the changing room, following closely behind the nurse. I did the same striptease I'd done two days prior, but this time, I did it without reservation. I stood there naked as the day I was born, shivering.

I shimmied into the blue-and-white gown and fastened the neck strap. I didn't even understand why I had to tie it, since from the spine down, my bare ass was exposed to the world. I contemplated taking the gown off and strutting down the hall completely nude; I didn't see the point of pretending the gown made me feel covered or less humiliated. Of course I didn't, though; I sat there in the open-backed smock with nothing but my socks on and waited to be called.

I lay down on the table, staring at the monitor displaying my name, age, date, and time, trying to keep my eyes open as wide as I could. I didn't want to fall asleep this time. I wanted to watch the procedure, to finally see for myself what was going on inside me.

I could feel a cool wind when the doctor lifted the tail end of my gown and flapped it open, leaving my ass cheeks and vagina out for anyone to see. I wanted to say, *What the fuck? Cover me up*, but my mouth wasn't in sync with my brain anymore. Thankfully, the nurse grabbed a giant blue piece of paper, or so it appeared, and draped it over me, finally restoring my dignity.

Oh no, I thought, as I felt my eyelids shutting just as Dr. Raymond lifted the large black scope that he was going to insert into my rectum. I fought the fatigue, popping my eyelids open. A few seconds later, I waited nervously for the doctor to apply freezing-cold gel. Then I felt the pressure of the large item entering me. It was an intense burning sensation followed by a hard pinch. Moments after insertion, I was out.

I don't know how long Dr. Raymond was trolling around inside me, but when I opened my eyes, he was standing over me, mumbling something.

"Ms. Beamon," Dr. Raymond repeated.

Ms. Beamon, I thought. *Why so formal? You've been more intimate with me than all of the guys I've dated.*

Instead I answered, "I'm awake."

"When you feel up to it, get dressed and stop by my office so I can go over the results."

What now? I thought. *If he didn't find anything, he would've said the test went well, go home.*

I rushed to get dressed, fighting off bouts of fatigue and dizziness. I was ready within ten minutes to face whatever he was about to say.

Dr. Raymond held up several photos, which evidently showed polyps in my colon. I saw the strange white bulges. They looked like harmless little mothballs to me, certainly not like something to get worked up about.

"We removed these polyps from your intestines during the exam. We'll send them out to biopsy them, but I don't think it's anything to worry about," said Dr. Raymond. "I wanted you to see them because it appears you are prone to polyps, which means you're going to have to be screened regularly."

Regularly, I thought. *I can't endure what I did last night that often. There has got to be a better way.*

"I'm going to order a pelvic and abdominal ultrasound so we can look at your other organs, in particular your liver."

My liver? What the heck is wrong with that now? I wondered. I should've asked, but I was mentally exhausted at that point.

"How are your GERD drugs working?"

"Well, it's been only a couple of days, but the burning has lessened. I can still feel everything I eat going up and down, though. I also get extremely sleepy at, like, nine PM; that's making it hard for me to function," I replied.

"I say continue with the drugs for a few months. If the symptoms don't get any better, then we will talk about other options," said Dr. Raymond. "I will have all of your biopsy results and scans by the end of next week. We'll talk then."

Easy for him to say, I thought. *He doesn't have to live like this. Better yet, he hasn't explained to me why I have to but he's ready to get rid of me.*

"Before I go, please tell me whether you will know or not if I have Cancer in the next five to seven days."

"I should," he responded.

I felt like he was shooing me out of his office. Dr. Raymond turned his back to me when he was done talking, as if all the questions swirling in my head weren't of any concern to him.

I'm such a coward, I thought as I sat in the chair and watched him walk away. *I should've asked him what's next if I have the big C. I also need to know how he's going to treat me, even if that's not the case, so I am no longer in agony.* I shook my head from side to side and continued to

think, *why did I not just speak up? It's my life we're talking about and I need to start getting real answers about why my body is falling apart.*

"I'm an idiot," I muttered as I meandered out of his office and down the hall into Bryce's waiting arms.

Bryce didn't pressure me to talk about what had happened with Dr. Raymond. He just waited for me to open up once I got into the car. The update spilled out of me in between my tears.

"How are you holding up?" Bryce asked.

"I don't know," I responded, still sobbing. "Dr. Raymond wants to run even more tests."

"For what?" Bryce snapped.

"He wants to look at my organs, my liver and stuff, now."

"Well, maybe it's just a precaution," Bryce said. "He has to run tests to figure out what's going on."

"I know, but how many?" I shouted. "Am I supposed to let myself become a human guinea pig? When does it end?"

"I don't know, baby," Bryce replied. "You have to be strong."

"I'm trying," I said. "I just can't stand waiting for the results of all these tests."

"I know, but there's no sense in getting all worked up until we know what we're dealing with."

We? I thought. I had never considered my illnesses as a "we" problem, but as I sat next to him in the car, it dawned on me that my shortcomings really affected both of us. Yet here he was, by my side, still calling us "we."

"You're one of the strongest people I know," continued Bryce. "I have no doubt you'll be just fine."

Chapter 4: Who's That Dude?

My paternal grandmother once told me that my long hair was what made me special; I didn't know I had internalized that belief until I went to brush my shoulder-length locks and clumps of them began to fall onto the bathroom floor.

What's going on? I thought.

I used the comb-over method employed by balding men to cover the growing thinning spot on the crown of my scalp and exited the bathroom.

"Look at this, Bryce," I called to him, digging through my hair to show him the two-inch-long patch that remained in the middle.

"At what?" Bryce asked, staring at my fingertips, trying to find the source of my irritation. "Calm down—it isn't that bad. Just put some hairpins in it so the long hair lies on top of the shorter hair, and you'll be fine."

I followed Bryce's advice, and it seemed to work. My hair stayed in place until I reached the wind tunnel formed by the tall buildings near my job. As soon as I turned the corner onto Sixty-Sixth Street and Columbus Avenue, I had to grab my hair to hold it down on top of the spot so no one would know my secret.

Maybe a multivitamin, a change in diet, or hair products would help the hair grow back, I thought.

For three months, I tried everything I could to save my hair. Despite my efforts, I was still shedding worse than any long-haired cat, and I was clueless about how to stop it.

Frustrated, I mentioned my hair loss to my primary care physician, Dr. Thomas, and my endocrinologist, Dr. Lee, who monitored my hormones. Both suggested my PCOS was to blame; they told me a shift in hormones, namely an increase in testosterone, could be the root of my problem. Neither of them offered a solution, though.

Great, I thought. *Losing my hair wouldn't be so bad if I wasn't a thirty-three-year-old woman dating a man with a wandering eye. Bryce's stayed with me the last four years, but it's been hard. I can't expect him to stay with me now that I am a bald, sickly woman.*

I was inundated with negative thoughts, which only got worse when I looked in the mirror in the bathroom in Dr. Thomas's office and noticed that at the same time I was losing my crowning glory, hair was starting to grow elsewhere, like on my chin and upper lip.

I'm Chewbacca the Wookie everywhere other than where it counts, I thought, as I stared at a long, curly hair taunting me from my jawline.

Funny, I chuckled, *when I was in elementary school, I hated the nickname Pippi, for Pippi Longstocking, because my braids were so long, they'd hit my shoulder and curl up. Now I'd give anything for that.*

I finally collected myself and went back out into Dr. Thomas's office; that's when he informed me that my hair loss might not be the last symptom of my PCOS. He delivered the news that it might also be difficult for me to lose weight or conceive a child. In fact, he suspected that the PCOS could be the cause of my having packed on twenty-five pounds since college, mostly in the form of a ring of fat around my belly. He also thought it might explain my miscarriage more than a decade earlier, during my junior year at Boston College.

Dr. Thomas was the only person, outside of my close friends and family, I'd ever told about the loss of my baby. He'd gotten it out of me when we were doing a full medical history. I was desperate to figure out when my body had turned on me, so I tried to recount every medical mishap that had happened to me since I was nineteen.

I truly had no idea what was happening to me that day in 1992, when I felt a stabbing pain in my belly that sent me stumbling forward, reaching for the hard, stiff living-room sofa. It was so intense that I couldn't even speak or cry out for help. I was overwhelmed by a stinging sensation between my legs that was followed by a sharp series of jabs inside my belly. Then I experienced a constant pressure in my bladder that made me feel like I had to go to the bathroom.

When the pain became unbearable, I grabbed the phone to call my doctor, who at the time was also my mother's doctor, but I couldn't compose myself enough to dial the number. I held on to the receiver, listening to the dial tone as I writhed in pain.

I tried to stand, but the pressure between my legs made it hard to rise up, so I just lay back down. Sweat began to bead on my forehead, and I felt moistness dripping on my thighs. It was warm and thick, not like water at all. I knew, in that instant, that I was losing my baby.

I didn't even get a chance to react to that when the contractions started. I shut my legs, hoping that would slow them down, but it just prolonged the agony. I dropped the phone on the bed next to me and spread my legs. It took just fifteen minutes for it all to be over; nothing was left of my child.

The revelation from Dr. Thomas that my miscarriage could've been caused by PCOS made me wish I had known that back then.

Maybe I could've saved my baby, I thought. *Perhaps I could've gone to the doctor more, taken some kind of pill that would've helped me, or, at the very least, maybe I wouldn't have punished myself every day since with the thought that losing my child was my fault.*

"Everything okay, Nika?" Dr. Thomas asked, realizing I seemed lost in thought.

"Yes, I'm sorry. I was just thinking," I responded.

"Well, all I can tell you is that Dr. Lee thinks you should continue to use the drugs we suggested to control your PCOS."

If the drugs work so well, how come the Provera and metformin didn't restore regular periods or my fertility, or stop the progression of the condition? I thought. *Clearly, they're not doing enough, because my hair is falling out by the handful where it's needed and growing where it shouldn't.*

Still, I took new prescriptions for a higher dose of both medications before I left Dr. Thomas's office and didn't express any of my displeasure.

As soon as I got back to Bryce's apartment, I unloaded on him.

"What happened?" he asked, right as I walked through the door.

"The usual," I responded. "The doctors say, 'Take more pills and you should be fine.'"

"So, the condition you have caused this? It's nothing new or more serious?"

"No, they claim it's all related," I snapped.

"Well, if it gets worse, we'll handle it," Bryce said. "In the meantime, we'll deal."

I figured Bryce was just giving me a pep talk about my declining appearance because he could see I was upset. But he adjusted.

He swept the bathroom floor twice a week, trying to keep up with the hair falling from my head onto the tile and the bath mats. He placed Drano at the side of the tub to unclog the drain and keep up with the volume of hairballs I was generating. It didn't take long, though, before I was tired of covering up my balding patch. I was unsure what to do until Bryce and I passed New Looks Salon on Washington Street in Hoboken about a month later. I decided right then to cut my hair.

"Can I help you?" asked the perky brunette, stepping from behind the counter, looking at me bewilderedly. I was the only black person in the shop and perhaps the only one who'd come in here for a haircut here in a while.

"You can. I need a haircut," I said. "I'd like to cut it about four inches long all the way around so it's in a short bob."

The brunette called a stylist from the back to come to the front of the store. I knew what she was going to ask her: if she knew how to cut **a** black person's hair.

Any real stylist can cut any type of hair, I thought. *One of the perks of having "good hair" is that I can get my hair cut just about anywhere.*

"Can you cut her hair?" she asked in the lowest voice she could muster.

"Do you have a relaxer?" asked the stylist.

"No, I don't, but you can just cut my hair like everyone else's," I sniped back.

"Okay, come on back," replied the stylist, accepting the challenge.

Bryce made a facial gesture that I understood to mean, *Are you sure?*

My response was a head nod signaling him to leave, that I would be just fine. "Come back in twenty minutes," I said to him, just before he walked out the door.

I enjoyed the feeling of warm water trickling across my scalp. I wasn't thinking about the amount of hair probably being washed down the sink. I just enjoyed the massage and the release of tension.

I rose from the hair-washing station already feeling lighter, even though not one strand of my hair had even been cut. The tickling of my wet locks on my shoulders ended seconds after I plopped down in the chair, when the stylist made her first snip. She grabbed a whole chunk of hair into a ponytail and made one decisive cut; there was no turning back.

I didn't look in the mirror as she parted and cut my hair at will. I glanced down only once, looking briefly at the hair spread out all over the floor underneath her chair. I didn't feel sad at all; I felt relieved—it was one less thing I'd have to think about every day.

The stylist spun my chair back around until I was facing the mirror and got a look at my new hair for the first time. It looked like a curly mushroom on top of my head, almost like I appeared in baby photos before my hair began to grow. I liked it. I was adjusting to it when I looked up and noticed that more than forty-five minutes had elapsed since Bryce had left me in the shop. While Bryce didn't complain about anything else going on with me, lateness was something that always got under his skin.

"Thank you," I said, as I began removing the black cape from around my neck.

"You sure you don't want me to blow your hair out before you go?" asked the stylist.

"No, no," I said, snatching the price ticket out of her hand and rushing to the front counter to pay.

I handed the receptionist $40 then flew out the front door and began scouring store windows for Bryce. I walked five blocks and didn't see him. Panicked, thinking he'd left me for being late, I patted myself down desperately, trying to find my cell phone. When I didn't feel it, I rifled through my pockets for change. I took a handful over to the only phone booth I could find and called Bryce's cell.

"Where are you?" he asked with irritation in his voice.

"I'm right down the block in front of Johnny Rockets."

"No you're not," he snapped. "I only see a dude standing there."

I stepped from behind the phone partition into plain view and again repeated my location.

"Is that you?" Bryce asked.

"You see me now. I'm at the pay phone," I said.

There was a strange silence on his end; then he said, "I see you. I'll be right there."

Bryce crossed the street and appeared to be surveying the area, like he was looking for someone else he knew.

"What's with you?" I asked, noticing he hadn't commented on my haircut or looked directly at me.

"Why didn't you let the hairdresser finish your hair?" Bryce asked.

"Why? Is it that bad?"

"It's not good," he said. "I hope you can fix it."

"I can," I replied, without having seen it since it had dried.

I struggled to keep pace with Bryce as we walked toward the Hoboken PATH train station. We got there just as a train bound for Jersey City was preparing to leave the station. The flashing yellow sign indicating the doors were about to close was on, so we hustled into the nearest car.

Bryce sat in a triple seat across from me as if he were ashamed to be seen with me. I tested him by getting up and sitting down right next to him. He slid a seat over and said, "Why didn't you let her finish your hair?"

I could feel tears welling in my eyes, but I wasn't about to cry in public. I slid back over to the farthest seat from him and remained there until we got to the Grove Street station. On the way, I glanced into the glass as we entered the tunnel and saw the dusty, matted ball of hair sitting on top of my head. I understood why he was embarrassed, because I was too.

As Bryce and I walked the mile to his apartment, I was careful not to get too close to him. He didn't seem to mind. He didn't slow down to let me catch up to him, as he usually did.

Bryce flung open the door to his apartment, leaving it ajar so all I had to do was push it when I got there. I headed straight for the bathroom and plugged in my curling iron.

I stood there, looking in the mirror, aghast at what I saw. It was the face of my two brothers, Randy and Taharka, staring back at me. I had always been told I looked like them, but with my hair this short, I was their spitting image, and that wasn't sexy on a woman. I'd never looked so androgynous before, never felt so plain and unattractive.

My hair is gone, and there's no way to get it back, I thought.

Instead of obsessing over my appearance, I got to work. For fifteen uninterrupted minutes, I straightened then curled my hair with the iron until it was a smooth bob, just what I wanted. The thick layers lay on top of the balding patch, covering it completely and helping it to blend in. I didn't look like a young black boy anymore; I looked like myself again, or at least a new version of me.

Hesitantly, I stepped out of the bathroom and into the hallway and awaited Bryce's reaction.

"You look great," said Bryce, the second I emerged. "I was worried there for a moment."

"Me too," I said, pulling him close to me and kissing him passionately.

When I released him, Bryce ran his hand across my smooth, short cut, which exposed my neck to fresh air for the first time in decades.

It's bouncy, sassy, different, I thought—*more like the attitude I need if I'm going to beat this crazy condition and whatever it has in store for me.*

Chapter 5: Too Hot to Handle

That morning began like many others; unfortunately, that had undoubtedly come to mean I began spilling the contents of my stomach shortly after waking up. I'd grown accustomed to a little blood coming out, so much so that I'd stopped mentioning it to my gastroenterologist or my primary care physician. However, this April morning, the blood flow wouldn't stop and I was really worried.

"I threw up blood again," I said, the instant Bryce picked up the phone at work.

Hearing the panic in my voice, Bryce asked, "You need me to come home?"

"I don't know," I replied, even though I kept thinking, *Yes, please come now*.

After five tumultuous years, Bryce knew the inflections in my voice and could tell my answer was a charade.

"Look, we're relaunching the CBS site, so I have to go to this meeting. I can't miss it, but I will take a cab and get back there as soon as I can. Can you wait?"

Bryce had just started at CBS a few months earlier. *I don't want him to lose his job*, I thought.

"Yes," I answered, unsure if that was truthful or not.

I vomited two more times during the hour-and-a-half wait; the amount of blood increased each time, making me think I'd ruptured something much larger than my usual cysts. I was shaking and growing weaker with each passing minute. I was preparing to walk the five blocks from Bryce's apartment to Harlem Hospital, when I heard the honk of a horn outside the front window.

He must've told the cab driver to keep the meter running and to wait for him, because he dashed out of the back of the vehicle and raced down the stairs into his apartment.

"You ready?" Bryce shouted as he burst into the living room, where I was laid out on the sofa, fully dressed, anticipating his arrival.

"Yeah," I uttered, stumbling to my feet while keeping one hand pressed to my belly, which was distended.

I hobbled up the stairs to the street level, pausing for a few seconds to settle the bubbling action in my stomach. Once it was under control, I dragged myself the short distance to the cab and flopped across the backseat, resting my head on his shoulder. Because I was too weak to walk, we drove the three blocks and two avenues from his brownstone over to Harlem Hospital. Bryce contemplated taking me to a private hospital, one that was familiar to us because of my many visits, but my writhing made him decide that the closest hospital was the best choice under the circumstances.

Bryce placed his muscular arms around my waist to support me as we strolled through the emergency-room entrance, which was illuminated by a MCDONALD'S sign. A podium turned into a security-guard stand greeted us a few feet from the door. The guard, who was conversing with a friend, barely looked up as we wandered past him in search of someone, anyone, who could assist us.

"Yes?" grumbled the nurse at the admissions desk, after she slid back what appeared to be bulletproof glass.

"My girlfriend has been throwing up blood, and she needs—"

Bryce couldn't even finish his question before the nurse chimed in, "Then she needs to go to the back."

I leaned on Bryce as he ushered me over to one of the visibly dirty plastic chairs in the waiting area; then he walked back up to the desk to tap on the glass. I couldn't hear what he was saying from where I was sitting, next to a motley group of people.

I'd just gotten comfortable when Bryce came over to me, helped me to my feet, and walked me over to a small door to the right of the window. We quickly reached the doorway to the nurse-practitioner's office. Bryce had barely gotten me into a seat when the receptionist told him he wasn't allowed in that area.

Bryce left me sitting in the room alone while I waited for the nurse-practitioner to return. When she did, I learned I was in the wrong room. Frightened and frail, I limped back to my feet and attempted to follow her. I braced myself, placing my hands on the wall, as I walked down the hall. Then I gently lowered myself down into the chair in her actual room.

The nurse-practitioner went over my information—name, age, and insurance—before she stuck a digital thermometer into my mouth. It beeped a few seconds later. She looked at the reading, and her demeanor instantly changed. She rose and exited the room with a sense of urgency that made me uneasy.

She came back a few minutes later and said, "You're running a fever, so I'm going to send you to the back to see a doctor right away."

"Can I let my boyfriend know I'm going to be here for a while?" I asked hesitantly.

"I'll go get him," she said. "I think you may be admitted."

The nurse-practitioner rushed out of the room to fetch Bryce, leaving me by myself to think about what a night at this hospital might be like. After reflecting on the condition of the waiting room, I had a strong inkling it wouldn't be pleasant.

"You okay?" Bryce asked, as he entered the room and placed one hand on my shoulder.

"Guess I'm going to have to stay here," I said.

"I can't stay with you," Bryce said. "I've got to get back to the office. The launch is in less than an hour, and I have no help."

"Oh, I know," I replied. "It's okay. I'm fine here."

Bryce placed a gentle kiss on my forehead, before an orderly came down the hall with the bed I was instructed to hop on for my road trip into the trauma-treatment area.

"Here is your jacket, with your cell phone and wallet. Keep it close to you," said Bryce. "Are you sure you're going to be okay?"

"I will," I answered, trying to inject as much confidence into my voice as I could.

"I'll be back to check on you as soon as I can."

I didn't look back as I was pushed away from Bryce, who was walking in the opposite direction. I clung to my possessions and tried to
 ease my nerves as I entered a large, open room with at least ten other people in it, separated only by curtains. I was placed into the last slot on the right, next to a woman who was bellowing about her pain. She was holding a towel around her bloody hand, moaning, rocking, and droning on and on about how long it was taking for someone to come and check her out. A nurse strolled up and pulled my curtain closed so I could no longer see the woman, but it did nothing to drown her out, nor did the machines, the incessant ringing of phones, or my own pain.

"Take off everything except your underwear, and put this gown on," said the nurse, tossing a gown onto my bed that wasn't in the plastic wrapping I'd seen at other hospitals, signaling it had been washed sometime in recent history.

"Where can I change?" I asked.

"There's a bathroom in the hallway," she replied, as she snatched the end of the giant curtain, pulling it so hard I thought she'd ripped it loose from some of its rings.

 She then took her other hand off her hip and pointed to the bathrooms.

The nurse didn't stick around to see if I needed help getting up or if I was even capable of it. She walked back over to the nurses' station in the middle of the room and left me to figure it out.

I managed to get to my feet, cradling the gown in my arms, as I slid along the wall into the hallway bathroom. I'd barely gotten into the gown and picked up my clothes off the floor, when I heard a knock at the door.

"Occupied," I shouted, thinking that would scare off the person, who'd started turning the knob. "I'm in here."

"I'm sorry, miss, but did you leave your jacket on the bed?" asked an unfamiliar male voice.

"Yes, yes, I did," I answered. "Why?"

"Some man just picked it up and walked away," the man said.

"What? Oh my God—my phone and wallet were in there," I exclaimed.

"Hang on, miss. I'll be right back,"

I cracked the door a bit to get a look at the man who'd just told me I'd been robbed in the emergency room. It was the janitor, pushing a trash can with a giant broom sticking out of its center.

I mustered enough strength to get back to the bed. My jacket was still sitting there. I let out a sigh of relief, thinking he must've been mistaken. But when I picked it up, my stomach, which was already doing somersaults, felt as if it were going to leap out of my body. My phone and wallet were both gone. I yelled out for one of the nurses to come over.

"Miss, someone took my wallet and my cell phone from my jacket," I said, as my voice cracked.

"Where did you leave them?" she asked, seemingly unconcerned with the answer.

"Right here, when I went to the bathroom to put on this gown," I said, tugging on it furiously.

"Well, I'm sorry, but we aren't responsible for your stuff," she replied. "If it turns up, we will get it to you."

I was starting to have a meltdown. I was shaking uncontrollably, ready to collapse in tears, when the janitor emerged.

"I caught up with the guy who took your things and got them for you," he said.

"I can't believe it," I said. "Thank you, thank you."

"It's okay, miss. Just keep your stuff underneath you from now on," he said.

"Can I give you some money or anything?" I asked, tears welling in my eyes. "Please let me thank you in some way."

"No, just keep a close eye on your things. People around here are sticky-fingered," he said as he slowly walked away.

Thank you, God, I thought. *This has been one of the worst days I've ever been through, until now. That man didn't have to help me, but he did, so thank you for letting him watch over me.*

I huddled in the fetal position, cradling all of my possessions, waiting for a doctor to come see me. An hour or so elapsed before one poked his head through the curtain. Speaking with a thick Indian accent, the doctor began by saying he'd reviewed the information the nurse-practitioner had gathered and thought it was best that I get whatever blood was left in my stomach out. The easiest way to do that was to insert a tube through one side of my nose and into my belly. While I didn't fully understand what he meant, I consented.

"I'm going to spray a little numbing medication on the tube and then insert the tube inside one of your nostrils," he said. "You may feel like you are choking when the tube reaches your throat, but rest assured you're not. You will be just fine if you keep swallowing. If it gets too rough, I will give you some water, but take only tiny sips."

"Okay," I replied, trying to process his instructions.

I took a deep breath as he began trying to snake the long plastic tube though my left nostril. Only about two and a half inches got in there before the pressure and burning sensation were so great that my eyes teared up. I tried to bear with him as he did his best to force the tube down, sending a sharper pain through the bridge of my nose and my cheek. Three times he tried, and three times he failed.

We're done here, I thought.

The doctor must have come to the same conclusion, because he pulled the tube out. He appeared frustrated, defeated, even. I guess I thought this meant he'd try some other method for clearing up the blood in my stomach. However, all he decided to do was to try the other nostril.

I braced myself, holding on to the thin mattress with one hand, as the doctor worked the tubing up into the nasal cavity. A few minutes later, I felt a pop and watched as another inch passed through the opening. It wasn't long before I felt a tickle in the back of my throat; an intense gagging feeling followed. I couldn't breathe or swallow, no matter how hard the doctor shouted for me to do so. I tried several times not to think about my heart palpitations and suffocating feeling and to just relax, but I couldn't.

I tugged on the tubing, yanking it out of me as fast as I could. It seemed like it took forever to get to the end of it—like that scarf trick magicians perform, except there was nothing cute or funny about this. Getting it out helped only minimally. I was left coughing and gasping for air. I couldn't hear the doctor's bitching over my own horrendous noises. However, when I calmed down, I could make it out.

"You shouldn't have taken the tube out," the doctor said, waving it around, despite the fact that the end was covered with snot and blood. "Now I have to get another one."

Does he expect sympathy from me? I thought. *I should jam the old tube up his nose and see if he doesn't try to yank it out.*

After cursing a few times, I grabbed some tissue from the box off the table to my left and wiped the tears from my face and the drippings of who in the world knew what from my top lip and cheek.

The doctor reappeared with a new tubing kit in plastic packaging. It stood out to me only because the previous one had been just in his hand, raw, with nothing protecting me from his germs.

I steadied my nerves as he snatched the tubing from its wrapping and approached me. I used Lamaze-style breathing, quick-quick then deep, to calm myself. This time I grabbed hold of the tubing and helped him guide it into my nostril. It reached the back of my throat quickly, catching me off-guard.

I closed my eyes and repeated to myself, "God help me. I have to do this. If you're with me and can hear me, help." I said it so many times, it started to sound like a mantra. It helped me muster up the courage to swallow the tubing into my esophagus.

I waved my hand, frantically gesturing that I needed something to drink to get the line all the way down. The doctor obliged, handing me a small cup of lukewarm water in a Styrofoam cup with a straw. The tiny gulps helped. I could feel the tube enter my stomach. It got there in spite of the fact that the numbing spray had worn off long before this attempt and the grating and scratching were difficult to bear.

The doctor wasted no time turning on the suction when he realized the tubing had reached its goal. I watched thick mucus mixed with blood fill a plastic container hanging on the wall beside me. I stared at the jar, trying to ignore the feeling that my insides were being vacuumed out through my nose. I started to feel a little woozy, like I was going to pass out, but then salvation: the doctor turned off the pump.

"We're going to have to admit you, Ms. Beamon," the doctor said. 'It looks like you still have some bleeding in your stomach. You see the bright red on top? That indicates an active bleed. I need to figure out where this is coming from, so I am going to order an endoscopy for tomorrow to find out exactly what's going on."

An orderly came within ten minutes to wheel me up to a room. I welcomed the move to an air-conditioned space with a TV, since the emergency room didn't have either amenity. I also wanted access to a phone, since cell phone use was forbidden in the hospital. That way I could let Bryce, my parents, and my work know that I'd be at the hospital for at least another day.

My bed rounded the corner into a giant room with three other beds inside. The orderly pushed me into an empty space over by a window with a view of the Schomburg library. An elderly lady suffering from asthma was in the bed on my side, closest to the door; directly across from her was a woman with cancer who'd come in for chemo treatment. The woman in the bed next to her didn't reveal why she was in, but the morphine pump she was hooked to revealed that whatever was ailing her was extremely painful.

I tried to be friendly, or as pleasant as I could be while stuck in a room with so many people. During my hospital tour, as I'd refer to it later, I'd been admitted to at least three other facilities in the New York City area, but there'd been no more than two other people in any room I had stayed in before.

This is the difference between public and private hospitals, I thought. *Public hospitals have too many people and too little space.*

The most annoying thing about sharing a room was answering a string of questions from the ladies while I waited for the TV-and-phone guy to stop by to turn them on.

"Where are you from?" the elderly woman in the bed closest to me asked.

"My parents live in Westchester, but I live in New Jersey," I answered.

"New Jersey?" the woman suffering from cancer questioned. "Then what are you doing here?"

"You didn't come all the way into Manhattan to come to his hospital, did you?" the woman in the bed farthest from me asked.

"No, I was at my boyfriend's apartment when I got sick," I replied.

"Oh, well, that makes sense," the elderly woman said. "Let me ask you something: You got insurance?"

"Yes," I snapped.

"Then get out of here," the woman with cancer said. "You can get better care somewhere else than you can get here. I've been here a few times, and I wouldn't keep coming back if I had options."

"Yeah," the woman in the bed farthest from me chimed in. "You need to get your man to get you out of here."

"I'll talk to him about that when he gets here tonight."

"We can't wait to meet him," the elderly lady said.

We'd barely finished our exchange when the telephone and TV man burst in, demanding advance payment in cash for turning on both the TV and the phone. As peeved as I was that the cost wouldn't be added to my bill, like it was at other places, I reached into my wallet and gave him the cash to activate the devices.

While I waited for them to be ready to use, I tottered over to the giant air-conditioning unit in the window. Although it was the end of April
, the temperature outside was already in the high seventies. Inside, it was about eighty degrees, and I needed cool air.

"Anyone mind if I turn on the air?" I asked.

All of the women responded no, so I reached into the control panel and pushed the HIGH COOL button. I expected it to kick right on, but nothing happened.

"Are you kidding me?" I said, not even knowing if the ladies were still listening to me. "We are going to sweat to death in here."

"It's been like this for days," the elderly woman said. "We gave up. I just thought you might know how to get that thing to work."

I can't believe this, I thought. *I'm sick and tired, but I'm not going to be able to sleep if I'm too hot. I've got to take my mind off this, because I'm getting really irritated.*

I wandered back over to my bed and picked up the telephone. Enough time had passed for it to be operational, so I picked up the receiver and ferociously dialed the operator to request that the AC be repaired. Right afterward, I began pushing the buttons on the keypad, trying to reach someone who could take my mind off the stifling heat and my roommates' mindless chatter. I don't know if I hit the buttons too hard or if the phone was already on its last legs, but the plate over the buttons popped off, exposing the phone's inner workings. I didn't care—I kept dialing.

When I heard ringing on the other end, I assumed it meant Bryce would pick up any moment, but a second later, I heard a snotty recorded message indicating I wasn't allowed to dial long-distance.

Since when is Manhattan long-distance? I wondered. *It's not a long-distance call; 646 is the new area code for Manhattan.*

Pissed, I dialed the operator back and demanded to be connected to the telephone people. Some guy picked up on the first ring.

"Yeah, telephone," the man said.

This is how you answer the phone at your job? I wondered.

"I prepaid for three days, but my phone doesn't dial long-distance. I was placing a call in the 646 area code, though," I responded.

"Well, it thinks that's long-distance," he said.

"But it's not," I sniped. "The phone is useless to me right now. Is there a way to get it to accept long-distance numbers?"

"No. I'll just bring back your money," he snapped back, slamming the phone down.

The telephone guy showed up a few seconds later, cash in hand. "Here's your fifteen dollars," he said, placing the money at the foot of my bed.

"Thank you," I replied in the nastiest tone I could summon.

The idea of being trapped in that hot box with no way to communicate with anyone was overwhelming. I decided to disregard the
 sign warning me against using my cell phone. I flipped open my silver Motorola Razr and called my job, my parents, and finally Bryce.

"They admitted me," I told Bryce, making my annoyance clear in my voice. "I'm in room 4C with, like, a million other people." I poked my head out from under the blanket to make sure the women didn't hear me, but they were oblivious; their faces were fixed on the tiny TV screen.

"What?" Bryce asked, not able to understand me because I was whispering too low.

"There are three other women in my room, and the AC, the phone, and my TV don't work; nothing here does. I really want to get out of here," I said. "Can you please just bring me something to read, some magazines, if you come visit me tonight?"

"I'll be there, baby girl," he replied. "Just try to get some rest until I get there. Do you need me to call your folks?"

"No, I took care of it," I answered. "Thank you, though. Just bring yourself, and that will cheer me up."

I hung up my cell and faked sleep in order to avoid talking about the soap opera playing on the only operational TV in the room. I'd actually drifted off, and had almost forgotten my miserable surroundings, when the sound of wailing woke me. It was the voice of a man, clearly in excruciating pain, crying out. He continued to holler for about an hour straight before he either passed out or finally got some relief; I didn't know which, nor did I really care.

I dozed again, only to wake up when Bryce came to check on me on his way home from work.

"You okay, baby girl?" he asked, sauntering into the room. His freshly dry-cleaned blue shirt was stained with a line of sweat down the center of his muscular chest. "It's hot as hell out there. It isn't much better in here."

"Who are you telling?" I responded. "I'm so, so glad to see you."

"Aren't you going to introduce us to your friend?" the elderly lady near the door asked.

She's just like Rose from the TV show 227— *always in someone's business*, I thought.

"This is my boyfriend, Bryce." I guess it was wishful thinking on my part to believe simply telling them his name would be enough for the women.

"So, Bryce, we hear you live around here," the elderly woman said.

"I do. I live a few blocks away," he replied, turning on his usual charm, which seemed to work on women of any age.

"You clearly came here from work; do you mind if I ask what you do?" she continued.

Bryce politely said, "I am a television web producer."

"Wow. Well, since you got a highfalutin job like that and are doing something with your life, you need to get out of Harlem. Ain't nothing going on here," she said.

"We told your girlfriend that too."

"Trust me," he said. "I'm working on it."

The women cackled to themselves as he pulled up a chair beside my bed and kept me company for an hour and a half, before hunger got the best of him.

"Well, at least I cooked last night," I chuckled. "There are leftovers in the fridge."

"Just get some rest," he said, placing his full lips on my forehead and kissing me good night. "I'll be back tomorrow. Love you."

Bryce's visit must've calmed me, because a few minutes after he left, I fell back asleep. I remained that way until a nurse came into the room at daybreak and woke me from a dead slumber. She checked my temperature and blood pressure. She also connected an IV to my arm to administer pain medication, which by that time I greatly needed. I didn't get up again until 8:00 AM, just in time to be wheeled down to the endoscopy room with my IV in tow.

Why did I bother to open my eyes? I thought, as the nurse stuck a needle into my IV and gave me a drug to put me to sleep for the procedure.

The drug was so effective that two hours later, I felt dazed and confused when I was jolted awake by a debate about whether Erica Kane should be acting the way she was—whatever the hell that meant. The ladies were huddled around the thirteen-inch barely color TV, holding their breakfast trays as they all chowed down.

Where's mine? I wondered as I hit the call button for the nurse.

The Trinidadian nurse flew into the room and asked, "What do you need, baby?"

"I just wanted to know about breakfast," I said, realizing my throat was so sore and scratchy, the lack of food might not be such a bad thing. "I just got out of a test, and no one left me a tray."

"Well, the guy who brings them is already gone," she replied. "Lunch is just a few hours away, though."

She turned away from me, after resetting my call button, and walked out of the room. I was too stunned to stop her or to say anything.

"You can have some of mine," the woman with cancer said.

"No, thank you," I replied, humbled by her offer. "I'll just wait for lunch."

The hours flew by as I read a book and then an outdated magazine Bryce had picked up at the only newsstand he had been able to find near the hospital. I stopped reading only long enough to talk to the cavalcade of doctors who Bryce led over to my bed to give me my endoscopy results.

"Ms. Beamon, how are you feeling?" asked one doctor, standing in front of a group of others, wearing white coats, who didn't look much older than I was.

"I'm a little hungry and sore," I replied.

"Well, it looks like you're going to need surgery to stop the bleeding, fix a hiatal hernia, and remove a few cysts."

"Do I have to do this right away?" I asked, desperately hoping he wasn't going to say yes and that I could leave that hellhole. 'I'd rather have my doctor do any surgery, if possible."

"You can if that will make you more comfortable," he said. "I can give you some medications to ease your symptoms until you get it done. You should see your doctor as soon as possible, though. Make sure to give him a copy of our report, or you will end up back here or another hospital."

"I hear you," I responded. "How soon can I leave?"

"I'll try to get you out of here tomorrow," he said. He was still talking when I got distracted by the other doctors behind him, beginning to talk and scribble stuff on their pads.

He brought them here to look at the freak, I thought. *He could've at least asked me first.*

Shortly after the group left, lunch arrived on a cart in the hallway. I listened anxiously as the orderly called out names and handed out trays to everyone but me.

"Excuse me, sir," I yelled out. "I haven't gotten food since I've been here, since yesterday."

"There isn't an order for you," he responded. "Let me check with the nurses."

I waited for him to come back, to bring me the good news that I was at least getting a cracker, some tea, anything.

"The nurse says the doctor has put you on a strict diet, but that food hasn't reached the kitchen yet, so your first meal will be dinner."

What the fuck? I thought. *I can't wait until dinner. I'm hungry right now.*

"What time is that?" I asked. By then I was so hungry that my headache was practically unbearable, and the pangs in my stomach were about the same. The only way I thought I could make it another three hours was to sleep. I knew dozing off would be difficult, though, since the temperature in the room had risen. My skin was moist to the touch, the hair closest to my scalp had started to curl up, and I was getting stuck to the sheets.

I adjusted over and over, flipping and changing position until I found a spot that made it possible for me to try to sleep. It took nearly an hour for the sandman to visit me. When I finally drifted off, I dreamed about all my favorite foods.

When I opened my eyes again, a tray of food was finally in front of me. Excited, I sat up and prepared to stuff my face with whatever was underneath the brown plastic lid. I recognized the scent wafting from it; it was pasta of some sort.

I can't eat anything tomato based, I thought. *The acid will eat right through my stomach, which is already so agitated it feels like a flamethrower is inside me.*

I frantically hit the call button, hoping to get the nurse's attention before the food guy escaped; I would take anything I could trade my dinner for.

"Yes, Ms. Beamon?" she shouted over the intercom, refusing to walk to my room this time.

"Can you stop the food guy?" I asked in the nicest tone I could muster, trying to get on her good side long enough to receive what I needed. "I think he brought me the wrong tray."

She didn't say anything else; she just sent the Jamaican man who had brought the trays earlier into my room.

"How can I help you, darling?"

"I can't eat this," I said. "The tomato sauce will hurt my stomach."

"Well, that's what I was told to bring you," he responded. He could see the anguish on my face and took pity on me. "Let me see what else I have on the stand. Maybe we can get you something else."

"Thank you," I replied. "I really appreciate it. I'm so hungry."

I took the other tray he handed me, with a fruit cup, milk, vanilla ice cream, chicken broth, and crackers.

Finally, I thought, *some stuff here I can actually eat.*

"Thank you, thank you, thank you," I exclaimed.

"No problem, darling," he said. "I'm just glad I could help."

I was wrong, God—there are *a few people in this hospital who are willing to help*, I thought before I lapped up everything in sight as fast as I could consume it. I was full, happy, and feeling much better than I had the entire time I'd been there.

Still, I thought, *I'm so glad I might get out of here tomorrow. Staying here has got to be worse than my illness itself.*

Chapter 6: Not Your Normal C-Section

This is not going to be easy, I thought, as my doctor explained my options for repairing the damage to my stomach and esophagus that had sent me to Harlem Hospital.

I could choose to get gutted like the catch of the day, allowing my entire midsection to be opened up from just under my breast down to my bikini line, or I could search on my own for a surgeon who could perform a laparoscopic Nissen fundoplication, a procedure in which a doctor would poke four holes in my belly, then insert tiny tools through them.

Of course I want the less invasive procedure, I thought. *But I don't know how to find a doctor, and if I delay too long I could get a whole lot worse.*

I didn't know what to do. Paralyzed, unable to make up my mind, I discussed my options with my parents and Bryce before dropping to my knees in prayer. The answer came to me right away.

The thought of tracking down a surgeon on my own was daunting, a reaction I was certain my current doctor had hoped for when he'd refused to refer me to anyone. Still, I knew the Nissen surgery was something I had to do. I wasn't going to allow myself to undergo a radical, medieval procedure simply because I was too intimidated to take charge of my own medical treatment.

I can do this, I thought. *After all, I do this every day as a part of my job. I'm a journalist. I know how to do research.*

I scoured the Internet and magazines, including *New York* magazine's annual list of the area's best doctors, looking for one with the skills to open me up. Then I asked my coworkers, especially those working in the medical unit at my TV station, for referrals. I compared the names on the list I'd gathered with online feedback from those doctors' former patients. Once I narrowed the candidates to the top ten, I called their offices for a list of former patients and a way to contact them for references. I treated my search as if I were gathering background information for a medical story at work. Less than a week later, I hit the jackpot.

My prayers have been answered, I thought, as I realized the name on the top of my list was Dr. Barry, a surgeon at NYU Downtown Hospital who not only was a pioneer in laparoscopic surgery but also accepted my insurance.

I nervously placed a phone call to Dr. Barry, fearing I'd sound like a blithering idiot as I tried to recite my symptoms and the procedures I'd already undergone. I thought perhaps my phrasing or terminology would be off or that he'd ask to speak to my current doctor, who would then scold me for going behind his back to find someone else to do his job.

This is crazy, I thought. *It's my body. I have every right to find the best doctor for me. I need to just suck it up and call.*

Despite my trepidation, I dialed Dr. Barry's number and blurted out my entire situation to his assistant.

"Miss," Dr. Barry's assistant said, "you are going to have to slow down and tell me again how I can help you."

"I'm sorry," I said. "I'm just nervous. I really need Dr. Barry's help."

"I understand," she said politely. "Why don't I have him call you?"

"Thank you," I replied, hanging up with my hands still shaking.

Dr. Barry called back in less than half an hour and listened patiently as I rattled on and on about my hiatal hernia, stomach dysplasia, GERD, and erosive esophagitis. I was close to apologizing for bucking what I thought of as proper medical protocol by calling him directly, when he stopped me.

"Sounds like you need a good surgeon," Dr. Barry said.

"I do," I said anxiously. "Do you think you can help me?"

"If your symptoms are as you described, I know I can," he replied. "First, I need to do some tests."

More tests, I thought. *You've got to be kidding.*

Dr. Barry interjected, almost as if he could read my mind, "I know you've probably done a lot of tests, but it doesn't sound like your doctors did the ones that I need to tell me exactly what is going on inside your belly."

Well, then what have the other doctors been doing all this time? I wondered.

"I get it," I said. "What do I have to do, and when do you want to get started?"

"I'd like to start as soon as possible," Dr. Barry replied. "First up, we'll get the best possible image of your stomach. To do that, you'll have to do a barium swallow test."

Sounds harmless enough, I thought.

"Once you complete that, I will have my secretary call you to tell you what else you'll need to have done," he continued.

I hung up with Dr. Barry, overjoyed that my misery could soon be over. I didn't even wait a minute; I dialed the number he had given me for West Side Radiology and booked an appointment.

Two days later, I arrived at the Midtown location with an empty belly and bladder. I flipped mindlessly through *People*, *InTouch*, and *Glamour* while I waited to be called into the back. I thought I'd missed my name, when I looked up, saw the nurse in the doorway, and realized she was announcing, "Nicka Beaumont."

I replied, "Yes" and walked over to the nurse silently, although I desperately wanted to yell out, *It's Nika Beamon, damn it.*

After stripping down and slipping into a paper-thin gown, I stood in the ice box of an X-ray room, in front of a giant table, awaiting instructions. A tech came in within five minutes, just as I started to shudder. I hoped he was handing me a glass of cocoa to warm me up; rather, it was a glass of a gray, chalky substance with a straw in it. It looked like the blandest milk shake I'd ever seen, so I took a sip.

The first taste wasn't so terrible, kind of like Maalox. *I can drink this*, I thought; *this isn't going to be so bad.*

The tech walked back into the room, interrupting my thoughts.

"Ms. Beamon, please hold the cup tightly," the tech said. "I'm going to tighten the belt around your waist so that you are snug against the table. The table will rotate into different positions so the barium can spread around. We are going to take different images as it does. If at any time you get nauseous, please raise your hand, and I will stop the table from moving and come into the room. If you start to choke, do the same. I will come in every few minutes to add a little more barium to your cup. Right now, it's the consistency of a broth. By the time you are through, it will be a little thinner than oatmeal. The straw will help you get it down. Any questions?"

I have a lot of questions, I thought. *How come you have to torture me to figure out what's wrong? How long is this going to take? Is it too late for me to change my mind?* Unfortunately, but I couldn't get them out before he left the room. *That's okay*, I thought. *I've been through worse than this. It will be fine.*

I lay with my head resting on the table, thinking, *I must look like the lady at the circus anxiously anticipating the next toss from the knifethrower.*

Helplessly, I waited for the tech's voice over the loudspeaker so I could quiet the chatter in my head.

"Sip, please," he said, as I listened to the X-ray machine fire up. "Are you all right, Ms. Beamon?"

I wasn't sure if he could even hear my answer, so I nodded, hoping he could see me through the glass. I figured he'd acknowledge my gesture, and when he didn't, I did the cheesy thing and gave him a thumbs-up.

"Take another big sip," he responded.

I did as he requested, swallowing more of the barium. This sip didn't taste nearly as pleasant as the first one.

We went through this drill over and over again, and he did as he had promised, adding more barium as time dragged on. At the fifteen-minute mark, the putrid smell was almost too much to take. I was full and feeling so much pressure on my waistline, I thought I'd pop like a pimple. The tilting table was like being on a ride at the fair, minus the fun. I was going to signal to the tech to stop, but I kept convincing myself to power through. But then, as if he'd read my mind, the tech told me, "You're halfway done, so let's take a short break, and we'll get started again shortly."

"Halfway?" I questioned.

The fluid buildup in my stomach was putting pressure on nearly every organ. I couldn't decide if I wanted to pee or puke. So the idea of consuming even more of the disgusting concoction was overwhelming.

You can do this, I thought. *You have to. Buck up.*

Somehow I was able to complete the test without spilling my contents from either end. I couldn't wait for the table to come to rest in the upright position and to be released.

"You're all done, Ms. Beamon," the tech said as he took the plastic cup out of my hand and sat it on the counter across from me. "Here's a glass of water. It should help settle your stomach. Take a few sips before you leave the room to get dressed."

The last thing I wanted to do at that moment was drink anything else, but I yearned to feel even the slightest bit better. So I drank as much of the lukewarm tap water as I could before making my way back to the changing room.

I slipped on my clothes slowly, trying not to further agitate my bloated tummy. It was hard to even button my pants at that point, because I felt like every time I fastened the button, it pushed the fluid out of my stomach and into my throat. I opened my mouth, hoping it would just pour out of me. I even contemplated sticking my finger down my throat and forcing myself to vomit. The only thing that stopped me was the fact that the bathroom was so close to the X-ray room and the waiting area, I feared someone would hear me.

I snatched one of the peppermint candies off the nurses' desk as I left the center. I figured it would settle my stomach, or at least my grandmother used to claim it was a miracle remedy. Within minutes, I began to think she was right. I was able to get back to my car and drive home, with the window down, of course, so the fresh air could calm the rest of my nausea.

It took me two days to fully recover and eat and drink normally. By then it was time for me to go for my second presurgical test, an esophageal motility study.

I didn't know anything about the test before I arrived. Turns out, it was good that I didn't. When the doctor came right in and told me that I was going to have to swallow a flexible tube, about one-eighth of an inch in diameter, by passing it through one of my nostrils and down the back of my throat, I almost fainted.

This sounds like the same shit I just went through at Harlem Hospital, I thought.

I contemplated leaving, but I remembered what the doctor at Harlem Hospital had said before I checked myself out: "We've stopped the bleeding and stabilized you, but it's unclear how long you will stay this way. You really need to have surgery."

Remembering that helped me settle down, at least until the doctor told me that over a period of fifteen to twenty minutes, I'd have to swallow repeatedly while he pulled the tube up and down my throat, getting readings on the muscle function of my esophagus.

This sounds like torture to me, pure and simple, I thought. *I'm at his mercy because I have to fix the big problem.*

Somehow I made it through the test, clearing the last hurdle for surgery.

Less than a week later, the day of my surgery, I got to Mount Sinai Hospital at eight thirty in the morning with Bryce by my side. We'd parked my car in the garage across the street so he could spend a little time with me, without worrying about feeding a meter, before I went under the knife.

Bryce waited patiently with me as I checked in at a small cubicle in the atrium area, even volunteering his information as my emergency contact. Signs on the freshly painted wall pointed out that the hospital had a wireless network. For people who didn't bring their computer, there were free ones set up. Bryce plopped down in front of one of the machines and did work while he waited for me to complete my paperwork.

"This is for you," I said, handing him a pager like the ones you usually get while waiting at a chain restaurant like TGI Fridays or Chili's. "The nurse said this will go off to let you know when I'm out of surgery. If you hand it back to them, someone will bring you in to visit me."

"That's cool," he said. "I'm kind of hungry, so I'm going to wait until you go in, then I'm going down to the cafeteria. Will this reach there?"

"I believe so," I replied. "The nurse said it should go off anywhere in the hospital."

"Well, I will be here when you get out," Bryce said, as he gave me a hug so tight he practically squeezed the air out of me. "It's going to be fine, baby girl."

"I know," I replied, placing a small kiss on his cheek.

I peeled myself off him, turned around, and headed toward the white door leading to the hallway to the anesthesiologist's office. I dragged myself each step of the way because my knees were shaking, making it hard for me to walk. It was just forty steps to the doorway, but it felt like miles away.

Well, I'm in your hands now, God, I thought, as I strolled down the sterile hallway to the office of the man who would be responsible for knocking me out and waking me up. *I just hope nothing goes wrong.*

As I reached the room, I was overcome by a thought: *A man whom I've never met literally holds my life in his hands. If he gives me too much gas, it's lights out; too little, and I will see and feel everything going on.*

I tried to think of any thought that would calm me down, but nothing seemed to work, so I began to pray silently to myself. I repeated the same thing I said every morning: *Thank you, God, for waking me up this morning*

*and laying me down to sleep last night. Thank you for my
ability to walk, to talk, to eat, to breathe, and to hear. All I
ask is that you continue to bless me and all those that
touch my life and that your will shall be done on Earth as
it is in Heaven. Amen.*

Dr. Martin walked into the room just as I finished
my prayer and introduced himself. He seemed pleasant
enough, especially considering that my insurance company
had forced me to call his office and ask if he
could lower his fee because it was more than they were
willing to pay. When his secretary said that wasn't their
procedure, I called my insurer back and informed them I
wasn't going to haggle with or piss off the man
responsible for keeping me alive, breathing, and pain free
during my surgery. Even though I wasn't happy that years
of illness had decimated my finances, I was willing to go
bankrupt if it meant I wouldn't die. I had no idea how
much Dr. Martin was going to cost me in the end; all I
knew was that I wanted to survive the surgery.

It took less than ten minutes for Dr. Martin to go
over a questionnaire with me and fill me in on the
anesthesia he'd be using. Right afterward, I was hustled
off into the preoperating room. It was so cold in there my
joints began to hurt; my fingers became stiff, and so did

my knees. Wearing only a gown, underwear, and those socks with the grips on them did nothing to cut down on the chill running through my body. I tried pulling up the flimsy sheet on the bed to use it to keep me warm, but that was futile. Just when I thought I'd have to just grin and bear it, a nurse noticed me shivering and brought over two blankets from a warming unit.

"Thank you so much, miss," I said. "I couldn't take the cold anymore."

"You looked like you were freezing over here," she responded. "I just thought I'd help."

"I was, so thank you for doing that and for paying me any attention," I replied, glancing over at the nurses' station, bustling with at least five other nurses, who didn't seem to notice me at all.

"No problem," she replied. "If you need anything else, press the call button."

Five other people lay in the beds near mine, each of us waiting for our doctor to come into the room to tell us when we'd be heading into the "carving" room. Mine came in first. Dr. Barry reassured me that I'd made the right decision in choosing him.

"How are you doing today?" Dr. Barry asked, as if today were just like any other day.

"I've been better," I replied, clutching my stomach.

Dr. Barry looked down at my hand placement and continued, "Trust me, you are going to feel a whole lot better after surgery."

I hope so, I thought.

I was wheeled into the operating room half an hour later, as the drugs pushing through my IV began to kick in. Even medicated, I could feel the frost in the operating room. I was almost certain it was cold enough to freeze the solution in the bag hanging over my head. I was shivering again within minutes and looking to finally pass out, when I heard a nurse point out that I'd forgotten to remove my belly button ring. I was dozing off, spread out on the operating table like Jesus nailed to the cross, when the nurse began to tap me.

"Ms. Beamon, how do you take this out?" the nurse asked.

I could hear her question, but I was too out of it to answer. My eyelids began to flutter as I fought to keep my eyes open. I saw only flashes of things, like the nurse tugging on the ring, trying to get it open. I couldn't feel anything, but I could see the frustration on her face. I fully expected her to climb up onto the table, straddle me, and yank it out even if it tore through my skin. But before I could find out what she was going to do next, I lost consciousness.

I was out cold, but I didn't dream at all, nor did I feel rested when I woke up in the recovery room several hours later. I was groggy, achy, and feverish. I looked down and saw a huge bandage covering my midsection and a plastic envelope taped to my chest; inside it was my broken belly button ring, which appeared to have been cut off, because it was in two pieces.

"Nika," said Dr. Barry, tapping me to make sure I was fully awake. "The nurse is going to bring you some Tylenol to help bring your fever down. You're going to have to stay in recovery until it does. I'll check on you in another hour or so."

I heard every word he said, but I didn't respond. I couldn't collect myself enough to do so. All I could do was mouth "okay."

My lips were so dry and chapped, they cracked and began to bleed when I tried to talk. Everything was starting to hurt, yet I was too weak to tell anyone.

"Open wide," said the nurse, sticking a disposable thermometer into my mouth.

I sat up, anticipating what it would read.

"Let me take a look," the nurse said. "You're down to 100; that's much better than the 103 you had an hour or so ago. You should still take these Tylenol."

I parted my lips and tossed the two pills inside. My tongue had so little moisture, they just stuck there until I took a big gulp of water, washing them down my throat.

I can finally get out of here, I thought. *This should get rid of the rest of that fever so I can be moved.*

"Visiting hours are over, but your friend has been waiting such a long time, I told him he could say good night," continued the nurse.

I glanced up at the clock and realized that almost seven hours had passed since I had checked in. As I lowered my eyes, I saw Bryce entering the room.

"How are you feeling?" he asked, as he sauntered up to my bed, wiping his eyes as if he'd just woken up from a nap.

"I'm fine," I whispered, almost unable to believe he had actually waited all those hours.

"Good," he said. "Then I'm going to give you my ChapStick, because your lips are mad crusty."

I cracked a small smile, then said, "You should go home and get some rest. You have to work tomorrow."

Bryce kissed me delicately on the forehead and whispered in my ear, "I'll be back tomorrow after work. Your parents said they'll be by in the morning. Get some rest, lady."

At that point, getting some sleep was all I wanted to do, so when I saw the orderly come in, release the brakes on my bed, and start wheeling me up to my room, I was thrilled. I couldn't really sleep in recovery. Between the frosty air, the sound of the monitors, and the nurses checking on me every half hour, I wanted nothing more than solitude and quiet.

Wow, I thought, as I was wheeled into my semiprivate room. *There's only one other person in here. Thank God.*

I could hear someone moving on the other side of the curtain dividing the room, but I couldn't see the person. After I was loaded into the bed and my legs were strapped into automatic circulation cuffs, a woman peeked around the curtain separating our beds.

"I'm Helen," the woman said.

"Hi, I'm Nika."

Helen just smiled, then dropped the curtain to block our view of each other.

Thank you, I thought. *I'm really not in the mood to exchange idle chitchat. I'm just hoping these drugs knock me out so I can get some sleep.*

I don't know exactly when I fell asleep, but I remember distinctly the moment I woke up. A stabbing pain in my bladder let me know that I was in desperate need of a bathroom.

I pushed the call button and waited for someone to answer me. No one called out, but I could hear the sound of breathing on the intercom, so I shouted, "Nurse, if you're there, I have to go to the bathroom."

"Use the bedpan," a nurse snapped.

Gross, I thought. *I'm not about to piss on myself or sit on a pot full of waste until someone decides to clean it up.*

Desperate, I tried to sit up so I could get myself out of bed. I quickly realized that having my feet strapped down and stitches in my gut made it next to impossible to do anything on my own.

"Excuse me," I shouted, hoping Helen was alert enough to hear my cry and respond. "Can you help me?"

Helen didn't answer. She just pulled back the curtain and slid herself to the end of her bed until her feet touched the floor.

"What do you need, dear?" she said in a motherly tone.

"I want to go to the bathroom, but I can't get myself up," I replied. "Can you help me?"

"Let me just get my wig, and I will try to help," Helen said.

Oh, she's an Orthodox Jew, I thought. *I wonder how she feels being stuck in a room with me.*

Helen shuffled over to my bed while holding her own gut and began removing the straps on the leg circulation cuffs. From there, she made her way up by my torso and helped me slide sideways out of the bed without moving my midsection.

"This is harder than I thought," I said, as I felt a strong tugging on all of my organs.

"Lean on me," Helen said.

Somehow, the two of us got me to my feet. However, the second I took a step, I felt a pop and saw a stream of blood shoot from my waist across the white floor.

"Are you okay?" Helen asked.

"I think so," I replied, as I fought back tears.

I didn't stop moving; I just continued more gingerly. I slid my feet along the cold linoleum floor, taking tiny steps toward the bathroom.

"Can you just slide that IV behind me?" I muttered.

Helen kindly obliged my every request, and I was able to relieve myself in a humane manner, rather than in the humiliating fashion that the nurse had suggested. After I was finished, Helen helped me back into my bed, put the cuffs back on my legs, then stacked toilet tissue on my wound so we could stop the bleeding. It would be two more hours before a nurse even peeked into the room to check on us.

"What did you do?" exclaimed the nurse when she finally entered.

"I must've moved somehow and hurt myself," I replied.

"You shouldn't have," she sniped.

"Maybe it happened as I tried to slide the bedpan underneath me," I said, making my sarcasm overwhelmingly apparent.

"Well, I will have the doctor check it out in the morning," she said.

Thankfully, I didn't see that nurse again the rest of my stay at the hospital, which was only two more days.

"How are you, baby girl?" my parents asked almost in unison when they popped into my room as I was preparing to go home.

"You ready to go?" my mother asked.

"More than ready," I replied. "I guess I'm going with you guys."

"No, Bryce said he and his mom will be here in a little bit to get you."

What? I thought. *I'm going to stay in his one-bedroom in Harlem with his mom?*

Bryce arrived less than an hour later with his mother following close behind.

"How are you doing?" he asked.

"I'm still here," I responded. "My folks say I'm going home with you."

Bryce glanced over at my mom and dad, then said, "I figured since your house has a lot more room than my place, my mom and I would stay with you. She's retired, so she can watch you during the day. I can take over for her at night."

Wait, we've been dating for more than a half a decade, and I've owned my house most of that time, and you've refused to stay with me more than a total of thirty days, I thought. *I've had to pack a bag and crash at your place three to four nights every week. It took my becoming an invalid for you to want to share my home.*

"Nika, did you hear me?" Bryce asked, realizing I had been silent for quite a long time.

"I hear you," I replied. "I was just thinking. Yeah, your plan is fine."

It took me a week to be able to get out of bed alone, two weeks to be able to walk the stairs in my townhouse without feeling like my organs were shaking, and three before I could swallow anything but liquid. Bryce and his mother were with me every step of my recovery. My parents relieved them on weekends, along with a rotating group of friends.

Nearly two months after my surgery, I was able to eat solid food again; that also cleared the way for me to return to work.

"You seem like you're back to your old self," Bryce said, as I rose to get ready for work for the first time.

"I'm feeling all right," I said. "I don't know how I will do sitting up for nine hours straight at my desk, but I'm ready to get out of this house."

"Good for you," Bryce said. "Hey, do you mind if I stay at my place tonight?"

"That may make my life easier," I responded. "It would make my commute a lot shorter."

"No, I meant just me," he said. "I have some things I have to do, like clean. It's been a while since I've been there more than a couple of hours; I've just been grabbing stuff and coming back here."

"Oh," I said.

Guess we've spent too much time together lately, I thought.

"You okay with that?" Bryce asked.

"Sure, you need some space," I responded. "No problem. I will be fine here by myself."

"My mom will stay with you."

"Right," I said.

Guess things are already going back to the way they were, I thought. *I just thought we'd finally made progress.*

Chapter 7: Do-over

No longer among the walking dead, suffering from chronic pain, coughing up blood, or running to the emergency room every few weeks, I was motivated to resume some semblance of a "normal" life. Sure, I was still taking more pills than my ninety-two-year-old grandmother, but I was up and functional. I was also lonely.

Bryce was laid off from his job at CBS less than two months after I recuperated from stomach surgery. Discouraged and out of work for more than six months, and with tensions rising at home, he decided to accept a job more than 250 miles away from me, in Virginia. He and I tried to keep things alive by traveling up and down the highway at least once a month, in addition to emailing and calling daily. Still, it wasn't the same. Bryce wasn't with me, and I felt his absence every day. Missing him was often accompanied by a fear that I would fall ill, that I was too sick to care for myself without his help, which I'd had now for nearly six years.

When I did see Bryce, he was different with me than he had been before. He was more standoffish with me, often treating me like I was delicate. Even the way he made love had changed. If he didn't seem like he was going through the motions, he was more reserved. He didn't try our favorite positions, like doggie-style or reverse cowgirl. It was missionary or nothing at all. His sudden lack of passion or even interest in me made me wonder, *If I don't please him anymore, how long will it be until he starts looking around again?*

I distracted myself from thinking about the deterioration of my relationship with Bryce by turning my attention to writing a third book. I began by thinking of a topic. I didn't have to look far; an ABC News special about why there are so many successful, single black women was all I needed.

I'm single, and so are a lot of my friends, but we're not complaining about it or obsessed with finding a husband, I thought. *We can't be the only ones. There have got to be other women out there who are happily single or at least not sad about it.*

I began crafting my book, looking for the most prominent single, successful black women I could find on the Internet. Then I wrote them an introductory letter explaining my desire to tell their stories to inspire other women to find joy in their lives, with or without a man. The first one to

respond was actress and comedienne Kim Coles. Her agent sent me her home phone number within a week, and I was well on my way to building a solid book proposal.

I turned her interview notes into the first story of the book. It appeared right after the only essay about my life in the entire project. Once those components were written, revised, and polished again, I got to work on the full book proposal. First up, I had to think of a name for my book. I began with the title *Alone, Not Lonely*.

The title and the concept immediately resonated with an editor at Chicago Review Press, Sue Betz, who bought it less than two weeks after I sent her the proposal. From the moment the contract came in the mail, I was on the clock. The entire project was then given a deadline of less than six months.

Able to stay up past nine o'clock for the first time in years, I typed interview notes, then drafted chapters, after putting in nine-hour days at work. Within four months, I'd finished a nearly two-hundred-page manuscript of the book that would forever after be known as *I Didn't Work This Hard Just to Get Married*.

As I flipped through the finished pages, I thought, *Am I as happy as these women? I have a boyfriend, but he's never with me anymore. I*
don't have someone to help pay the bills, take care of me, or provide daily encouragement when I am sick, which is all the time. I'm exhausted, nearly bankrupt, and scared constantly. I don't know how bad my illness will get and whether someone will have my back if I can't do it for myself.

I spent the next month and half revising the pages of my book so they were revised enough for the publisher to accept them and give me the second half of my advance. I spent the month after that making the changes my editor wanted. Finally, after the project couldn't be tweaked any more, it was ready to be sent out for advance reviews.

It wasn't long before interview requests flooded in, quickly making me one of the poster children for sassy, secure, single black women. Blurbs, quotes, and small excerpts filled the pages of nearly every major black magazine and newspaper and were plastered on the web, along with a picture that made me look like the epitome of health.

I knew I wasn't supposed to share any of the real trials and tribulations of my long-distance relationship or my struggle being single and sick. My job in marketing the project was to be positive and inspiring, even if that meant being misleading about my own experiences. I consoled myself with the thought that my story wasn't in the book, so I was really representing my female subjects, who were perfectly happy being on their own.

I'd blathered on so much about the book prior to its official
release, on Friday, May 1, 2009, that I was sick of hearing myself drone on. All talked out, I walked into the Gaslight Lounge in Manhattan's Meatpacking District fifteen minutes after the start of my private book-launch party.

I stood idly by in the corner of the room, near a display containing about a dozen copies of the book, sipping on my Coke, which I desperately wished had a splash of rum in it. Balancing on my big-girl shoes, I tugged on my uncomfortable dress, with a large black belt accenting my absent waist, while friends old and new, coworkers, book-industry associates, and a newspaper reporter buzzed around the room. I watched as they sucked down as much of the top-shelf liquor as they could and nibbled on the food spread, seemingly oblivious to my presence.

I was starting to believe I could simply slip out unnoticed, when I glanced over to the bar and saw several copies of *I Didn't Work This Hard Just to Get Married* lying on top of it. It appeared that several of the people attending had purchased the book prior to their arrival so that I, a pseudocelebrity, could sign it. Humbled, I collected myself, bracing for the long night ahead.

"May I have your attention?" said the bar manager. "I think your hostess, the woman of the hour, would like to say something."

I don't know where he got that idea, I thought, fidgeting and hoping everyone would just ignore the booming voice on the public address system.

Mortified, I stood cradling my cup and refusing to move. After a couple of minutes, the bar owner put the microphone down, defeated. The music came back on, convincing me that I'd dodged the uncomfortable situation, until I heard my father begin to speak.

"Thank you all for coming," he began. "I'm proud of all of my children: my two sons, Randy and Taharka, and most of all, my daughter, the author and the reason we are all here tonight."

He continued to speak until he became overcome with emotion and passed the microphone to my mother, Gloria. She was short and sweet, and never took credit for being my copy editor.

"I would just like to say I'm sorry my husband talked your ears off," my mother joked. "I'm glad all of you could be here to share this special moment with my family. You don't know how much it took to get here, but we're grateful."

I have to say something, I thought, as the crowd of people looked around to see who was going to pick up the microphone next.

"Thank you all for being here," I said. "I didn't plan to speak tonight, so I will simply say I appreciate the support. Now eat and drink up. I've already paid for everything."

I concluded my brief speech as fast as I could and retreated back into the corner. I watched from afar as my guests reveled. Bryce was one of them. He'd moved back from Virginia just weeks earlier.

Look at him, I thought, staring at Bryce across the room. *He's moved back to New York, but he's still ignoring me.*

I feigned smiles for photos and made idle chitchat while signing books, intermittently glancing over to see what Bryce was doing and with whom. I watched as he played the social butterfly. He flitted from woman to woman until he stopped at an acquaintance of mine. He bent over and began whispering in Kristin's ear. Although I couldn't hear what he said, I knew it wasn't casual chatter between two people who barely knew each other. For a moment, I considered walking over and confronting him, but I knew it wasn't the time or the place. So I just stood back and observed.

It didn't take long for Bryce to look up and realize I was watching him. He flashed me a smile, then made his way over to me.

Clearly intoxicated, he said, "You having a good night, baby girl? This is your night."

"It's going," I snapped, as Bryce gave my cheek a wet kiss, which I promptly wiped off.

"Let's take a picture," Bryce said, throwing his arm around me and pressing his cheek to mine.

I forced a smile until I saw the flash on the three cameras pointed at us go off. Afterward, I broke free from his grasp and stood beside him with my arms folded.

"I'm going to grab another drink," Bryce said, aware of the tension between us.

"Go and enjoy," I said. "I'll catch up to you in a bit."

I checked my cell phone for the time, counting down the minutes until the evening's festivities were over and I could take off my four-inch heels and revert to my laid-back self. Finally, the witching hour, one o'clock in the morning, arrived.

With Bryce, his childhood friend, and his college roommate in tow, I tiptoed all the way down five blocks to a diner to eat, something I'd neglected to do all night. I collapsed into the booth, immediately slipped off my shoes, placed my sneakers on, and breathed a sigh of relief.

Thank God the night is over, I thought.

The next few weeks were a blur, filled with magazine and newspaper interviews, as well as Internet- and broadcast-radio segments, including the *Tom Joyner Morning Show*. My head was swimming with dates, times, and phone numbers for all the places I needed to be and with whom I was supposed to speak. The chaos made it easy for me to overlook Bryce's suspicious behavior with Kristin and the cavalcade of symptoms ravaging my body, making me feel run-down.

Exactly one month later, it was time for my first author appearance, at the iconic Hue-Man Bookstore on Frederick Douglass Boulevard in Harlem, which had hosted Hillary Clinton, Angela Bassett and Courtney Vance, and too many other celebrities and dignitaries to mention.

I'd had only five hours' sleep when I dragged into work. I put in a full day and was preparing to run out the door and hop into a cab, when my phone rang. It was my mother. It wasn't unusual to hear from my mom, especially at work, but she was due to meet me at the bookstore in less than an hour, so I knew that this wasn't an ordinary call.

It only took a few soft-spoken words to change my day, outlook, and my priorities.

"What's wrong?" I asked, hearing a bizarre melancholy in her voice.

"Your uncle George died. He was found dead alone in the bathroom of his studio apartment in Brooklyn," she said. "Your father is on his way out there to do what he does best—take care of everything—so he may or may not be back in time for your book signing."

"What?" I asked, trying to process the news. "He seemed okay at the book-launch party. What happened?"

"They don't know yet," my mom replied. "I'm sorry this is happening today."

"I don't think I should go to the signing," I responded. "I can meet you guys in Brooklyn."

"No, don't cancel your event," my mom said forcefully. "You father and I wouldn't want that, and neither would your uncle George."

I still think I should cancel, I thought as I hung up the phone.

I had an internal debate for a short time, then shook off my shock and got into a yellow cab to go to the bookstore. I was running about five minutes late, but I didn't care.

I walked into the venue and straight to the back, where I was ushered into a private room while the owner waited for a crowd to build. I didn't pack the place like famous authors generally do, but I had a solid twenty-five people there, most of whom weren't friends or family, so I was pleased. I paced around the room, trying to get my thoughts off my uncle George and back on my presentation. However, it seemed futile.

My uncle George and I weren't particularly close, but he was always there. He was at family barbecues in the summer and as many holiday dinners as my dad could stand, and he was in my car the day we drove back from my paternal grandmother's funeral.

My memories of him flooded in as I exited the back room, ready to take center stage.

"Are you ready?" the bookstore owner asked.

"As ready as I'm going to be," I responded.

I walked to the table in the front of the room with my notes in hand and was stopped dead in my tracks when I saw my parents sitting in the first row of the audience.

"Good evening," I began. "Thank you all for coming, especially my parents. I can't believe you came to my signing, considering everything going on. I know this is the last place you want to be, but I'm glad you made it. All of you as well," I said, as I glanced around at the crowd.

The rest of the night went as I had originally planned, except, of course, for the nagging thoughts in the back of my mind.

Shouldn't I be wallowing in sorrow for my uncle? No, he wouldn't want that, I thought. *He was always about living life, finding a reason to let out his raspy laugh, and finding a way to escape the harsh realities of life by never growing up.*

Uncle George was sixty-eight when he died, but if

anyone asked him his age, he'd always say he was seventeen. I never asked him for the truth, but I know he was seventeen the year before he went to jail for the first time, before he had five children he barely saw, before his abusive marriages, drug addiction, and family estrangement.

It didn't occur to me until I got home after that long day that maybe he'd said he was still seventeen because he'd wanted a do-over, a second chance to alter his life path. *Who doesn't?* I thought. *I know I do. Perhaps I'd be healthier, have a faithful boyfriend, and be a best-selling author this time.*

I didn't speak to my parents about my revelation; I kept it to myself. I simply composed myself and made it through my next series of book signings. A sense of grief didn't come back to me until I sat down at my computer the night before my uncle George's funeral and an essay poured out:

[[Q]]

Grief is a funny thing, not like a joke someone tells you that leads to a hearty chuckle; rather, it's an odd emotion that evokes a varied reaction in each and every person it touches. It can unexpectedly paralyze some, making it hard to move, to talk, or to think, unless it's about wishing you were the one who passed away instead of the person who did. Loss can make others feel numb, like they are in a fog or a haze and their thoughts are a muddled pile of gibberish.

Or grief can make you feel the way it transformed me. It left me remarkably serene about my uncle George's passing. I knew that his torment here on Earth was over, and that's a relief. I know that in the end he knew that he was loved for exactly who he

was, and not for the person we wished he could've been. I am also a person of faith, so I believe he's in a better place, and that, if nothing else, allowed me to sleep easier. And I was at peace because I had so many wonderfully entertaining stories about how he touched my life.

There's the time he didn't believe me when I said I only make one stop for every four hours of driving, so he chose to drink a wine cooler when I made a pit stop coming from Virginia to New York. My brothers took a bathroom break because they were well aware of my rule, but he did not. So when we were eight hours into our trip, stuck in traffic near the George Washington Bridge, he had to beg me to pull over because he couldn't hold it anymore.

At my father's fiftieth-birthday party, I had to banish him to a chair in the spare bedroom because he wouldn't stop hitting on women at the party. As I iced a homemade carrot cake, I could hear him calling my name, asking to be allowed downstairs with everyone else and promising he'd be on his best behavior.

No matter how many times he was put out of my parents' home, my father always invited him back for the next party, barbecue, or holiday, and he always came. I think he envied the life my father had made for himself, wanting a piece of it for himself, even if he could only have it as a visitor.

Uncle George was a character. He was outrageous and audacious enough to be himself no matter what anyone else thought, so his passing has also left me terribly curious. I began to wonder this morning if I have these two crucial personality traits. If I have the courage to be who I want to be and not the person others expect.

[[Q]]

I put my essay away and rose for my uncle George's funeral that Saturday morning with no more sorrow in my heart.

I reached the modest funeral home on West Forty-Third Street just in time to see a prison van pulling away.

I guess one of his sons was allowed to come out for a few hours to say good-bye, I thought as I climbed the stairs to the second floor, where my uncle's body was on display in a simple room. An easel with pictures of him was to the right of his casket, and a poster board featuring one of his essays was on the left.

I didn't even know he was a writer, I thought as I passed the essay on my way over to him, in an open casket. Uncle George was wearing a navy suit, no doubt one that my father had purchased or given to him, like so many before that. His hair was close cropped and natural, not in the Jheri curl or wave style he'd worn most of my life. He looked handsome—adult, even—for the first time in a long time.

I peeked briefly at him before slinking through the back door of the room to take a seat near my uncle and his wife, who'd driven up from Virginia, along with my father's sister. I scanned the room, trying to identify most of the people, but I couldn't. Sure, there were the usual suspects, the relatives who always showed up for major gatherings. However, everyone else was a virtual stranger to me.

Painfully absent was my father's oldest brother, Jimmy. I'd halfheartedly thought he'd show up, even if it was to gloat that he was alive and my uncle George was dead, although I knew his presence was only a remote possibility, since he hadn't been seen or heard from since Christmas 1993. My wishful thinking was spawned by a desire for him to provide some comfort to his remaining siblings about his whereabouts. I knew my father had wondered many times whether Jimmy was still alive.

I was lost in my thoughts until Bryce entered the room, decked out in a blue Nautica suit perfectly tailored to his body.

"What are you doing here?" I asked. "You didn't even know my uncle."

"I know," he replied. "But I know and love you, and I came to support you."

My father served as the main eulogizer at the service. He stood teary-eyed over his brother's casket, recounting his memories of my uncle.

I listened intently as he described their complicated relationship, filled with strife, as if that were the way all siblings should behave. Nonetheless, his love for Uncle George shone through, causing me to wonder if my uncle had known he didn't need a second chance at life at all, that he had a pretty good one, if only he'd stopped and taken stock.

My father, overwrought with emotion, called on others to share their memories of my uncle so he could collect himself. Even though two of my uncle's five living sons were sitting just feet from him in the first two rows, neither moved. Desperate, my father looked around and locked eyes on me. He invited me up to say a few words, a task I reticently accepted.

I filed past the two older men who by birth were my uncle's sons to the front of the room. I stood looking out at them, brow furrowed, holding my tongue as I prepared to speak. Before I could open my mouth, my brothers joined me, standing within eyeshot and helping me to calm the furor stirring inside. I shook each of their hands, then turned to the crowd and told them about my uncle George's reluctance to be any age other than seventeen.

"You taught me to make the best out of the time I'm given so I don't ever long for a do-over," I said as I looked at the remains of my uncle.

With that, the tears that had eluded me since I'd gotten word of Uncle George's passing began to flow forth.

Chapter 8: Spoonful of Sugar

Longfellow wrote: "Into each life some rain must fall."
Well, my life was the exception; it was becoming a deluge
of bad news. Just weeks after my uncle's sudden death, my
father began to suffer from mysterious stomach pains.
He'd had something similar before, so I wasn't initially
alarmed, but when he conceded to my mother that he
couldn't stand it anymore and needed to be rushed to the
emergency room, my entire immediate family took notice.

I sat by the phone, waiting for my mother to call
with an update; she'd become the family telegram service,
delivering the news of births, death, sickness, and so on.
An hour passed, then two, three, four hours, before she
called to alert me that my father had been sent home by the
doctors, who had found only a severe case of acid reflux.

Gas, I thought. *I was worried about him having
more than an upset stomach. I'm becoming paranoid, I
think—all of my crazy medical problems have made me
project onto other people.*

My father's symptoms returned with a vengeance a few days later.

Are you kidding me? I thought, as my mother explained that she had rushed my father back to the hospital. *Did they actually misdiagnose him?*

The doctors at Westchester County Medical Center didn't know what was wrong with my dad, but after he'd spent two hours in the emergency room, they knew one thing: my father needed to be admitted. Unfortunately for him, the only thing they knew to do was to give him a gastric lavage, an antiquated process to pump blood out of the stomach through a tube in the nose—a procedure with which I was all too familiar.

Day after day, my father languished in the hospital, unable to eat solid food of any kind, as doctors performed a battery of tests. None of them gave him much of a clue as to what was going on.

The days stretched into weeks as my father wasted away, losing at least thirty to forty pounds. His cheeks were sunken, his eyes bulging, and the skin on his once-muscular arms hung loosely. His rib cage was apparent, and his stomach caved inward. He failed to look like the towering figure who'd intimidated me in my youth. Rather, his stark white hair and drooping frame made him look delicate.

On June 25, our wait for some sort of status report came to an end. My mother and I huddled around my father's hospital bed as the doctor delivered what we hoped would be a positive plan of attack.

"We believe you've got a bacterial infection of your intestines. The best solution is surgery," the doctor said. "We'll go in and remove the infected portion of your intestine and give you a colostomy bag while your intestines heal. We should be able to remove it in a few months."

My father squirmed on the edge of the bed, then immediately snapped, "No. No surgery."

The doctor turned to my mother and me to plead his case, but my father interjected, "I'm not going to wear a colostomy bag."

"This is the best option for you to get rid of the infection, alleviate the pain, and allow you to go back to eating solid food. Without it, the infection could spread throughout your intestines, making them septic."

His damn pride is going to kill him, I thought.

I chased the doctor out of the room and down the corridor to the nurses' station, then asked, "Are there any alternatives to surgery?"

"We've tried every antibiotic we have, and they don't seem to be working."

"Well, let me ask you a different question, something a little offbeat," I continued. "I recently had a Nissen fundoplication for my gastrointestinal issues. I've also had polyps in my colon and been given a host of drugs—including Protonix, omeprazole, Reglan, nortriptyline, Nexium, and Citrucel—for my issues. Is it possible that what I have and what my father has are the same condition or related?"

"Genetics do play a role in most diseases, so that's not an odd question, but there is no way I'd know unless I saw your medical records," he replied. "Did your doctor do genetic tests or tell you exactly what condition you had?"

"No," I responded.

I can't believe I never pushed my doctor for an exact diagnosis or an answer to my underlying problem, I thought. *Maybe I could help my father right now if I had; my suffering would not have been in vain.*

"It seems like you've been through a lot," the doctor continued. "Your dad's about to get a lot worse unless he gets the surgery he needs. I've given him the best medical advice I can."

"Let me talk to him to see what I can do," I said, turning to head back to my father's room.

I knew the truth could be a bitter pill to swallow, so I figured a healthy dose of sugar, which meant my being pleasant and optimistic,
would help my dad absorb the news that he needed an operation. I settled my nerves and reentered his room with a calm look on my face. I laid out my best persuasive argument for surgery to try to get him to comply, but it was fruitless.

"I'm not going to have the surgery. I don't need it," exclaimed my father. "I will just keep trying the antibiotics. The doctor who was here yesterday says there is a stronger one I can get through an IV. I'd rather try that. If it doesn't work, then I will think about surgery."

Yeah, right, I thought.

I wanted to shake the stubborn streak right out of him, especially since I knew if this had been a medical decision I had to make and he'd been present, he'd have tried to impose his will to get me to go along with the surgery. Hell, he'd done just that on many occasions.

Defeated, my mother and I exited my father's room to grab a bite for lunch and, more importantly, allow him to reconsider his decision. I'd just calmed down in the elevator when we exited into the lobby and saw that all of

the televisions had a banner announcing breaking news:
MICHAEL JACKSON RUSHED TO THE HOSPITAL
UNCONSCIOUS.

Shit, I thought. *I can't deal with this today.*

A few minutes later, as I suspected, my cell began to ring. The number flashing across the screen was my job.

"Aren't you going to answer that?" my mother asked as we sat down at an Applebee's a few blocks from the hospital.

"No, it's work," I replied. "I know why they're calling."

"It seems important," she continued. She then looked back down at her menu.

"They want me to come in to work on the Michael Jackson story."

Just then, I looked up and saw a new headline flash across the television screen just above our heads: MICHAEL JACKSON DEAD AT 50.

I can't believe it, I thought. *He's dead.*

A beep on my cell phone reminded me to check the voice mail.

"Nika, please call the news desk," the assignment desk manager said. "We're looking for writers to come as soon as possible to work on the Michael Jackson story."

I guess I have to call, I thought. It wasn't like I didn't want to work on the story; it was one of the biggest of my career. As one of the only black writers left at the station, I was almost obligated to cover it. Then I thought, *I just can't handle a long news day while dealing with my father's illness. I can go in to the office tomorrow. Michael will still be dead.*

"Hey, it's Nika. I'm at the hospital with my father today, but I can come in first thing tomorrow morning. Just let me know what shift," I told my boss.

"Is everything okay?" my mother asked as I hung up the phone. "Are they upset you aren't coming in? I can go back to the hospital by myself."

There is no way I'm going to work right now, I thought.

I didn't respond to my mother, and she didn't repeat herself. I think she knew what I was thinking.

Uncharacteristically, we finished our lunch in near silence. My mother began to speak only when I took out my massive pill case and swallowed the contents.

"How are you feeling?" she asked, staring at me to try to gauge how I was holding up.

"I'm okay," I replied, not wanting to generate any additional worry for her.

The reality was that the pain, nausea, and fatigue that had plagued me for years had returned, though they were milder than before. I distanced my thoughts from my symptoms, chalking them up to stress over losing my uncle, my father's health, and work.

I quickly changed the subject, telling my mom about my conversation in the hall with my father's doctor.

"There is a bit of good, or should I say interesting, news," I began. "Dad's doctor says there's a chance that what he has and what's been wrong with me are related."

"That *is* interesting," she replied. "When this is all over, maybe we should get genetic testing or something done."

"Let's get Dad through this first, and then we'll tackle that."

My father writhed in pain for another week, repeatedly refusing to have the surgery. It didn't help that the anesthesiologist told him that propofol—the same drug that had allegedly killed Michael Jackson—would be used to sedate my dad. He did agree to the infusion of a powerful antibiotic, the very same one his gastroenterologist assured my mother and me wouldn't work.

Anxiously we waited, expecting my father to take a turn for the worse. Yet, two weeks after he started the IV antibiotics, he started to get better. His skin changed from a dusty gray color to its usual shade. The pump in his stomach, which had spent weeks suctioning out black and deep-green mucus-like fluid, was now removing nearly clear liquid from his body. Even better, his appetite had returned, although his food consumption was still restricted.

The antibiotics were working, and his primary gastroenterologist didn't know why. His doctor wouldn't admit that he was wrong, that he might've misjudged my father's case. Despite my father's insistence that he get an apology, one never came.

The doctor should say something to us for scaring us, making us think that we should be preparing ourselves for my father's passing, rather than his recovery, I thought. *I don't understand why doctors can't admit they don't know or that they are wrong. Perhaps I should follow my father's example in the future and go with my gut and fight for my health, no matter what the doctors say.*

Chapter 9: Stevie Wonder Can Drive

I'd waited nearly eight years for Bryce to finally share a home with me, yet it took less than a year of cohabiting for me to want to flee our townhome. Besides his disappearing acts, which included leaving me on the sofa in a bustier holding a book full of boudoir photos I'd taken for him and bound in a book for Valentine's Day, Bryce was increasingly more secretive and distant.

I'd grown accustomed to him having occasional side flings, and I even stood behind him when he had a paternity scare with another woman, but I wasn't prepared for what I stumbled across on his computer one April morning.

I figured Bryce had files neither I nor anyone else was supposed to view when he purchased a computer that wouldn't even boot up without a thumbprint and a password. However, I was flabbergasted when I strolled over to it, open on the guest bed in our spare room, and found the cursor hovering over his photo folder.

My conscience told me not to do anything other than move the arrow over to the START button and shut it down. My gut told me something entirely different. It directed me to click on the folder to see what was there. I gave in to the latter impulse.

The first file revealed pictures of him locked in an embrace with a Kristin, the same acquaintance he had seemed too cozy with at my book party.

What the fuck? I thought. *He's been parading her around Harlem behind my back. How could he? How could she?*

I began to shake as I continued to open file after file, uncovering more and more women I knew nothing about. There were a few I thought he'd ended his association with years prior; instead, there they were, staring at me, locked in embraces with him. The most shocking were the photos of the other women with his family and friends at weddings and parties he either had never told me about or hadn't invited me to.

He humiliated me, I thought. *He showed them off and left me in the house. I'm good enough to help with his work, to pay bills, and to give him a home, but when he wants someone to have a good time with or show off, that's not me. How could his family and his friends not tell me? They helped him make a fool out of me.*

Furious, bewildered, I couldn't speak.

I snatched my cell phone off the bed and laid into him with a tirade that began simply: "I'm going to ask you something, and I want you to answer me honestly. Did you hook up with Kristin?"

"Yes," he replied without a hint of remorse in his voice. "Have you been going through my things again?"

"You left your computer on. I went to turn it off and saw files called Harlem, Don's Wedding, and Thanksgiving—all places and events you told me you went alone. It struck me as odd that you would have all these photos and never show them to me. So, yes, I did—I went through them. That's not the point, though, is it? All of these women behind my back—Tiffane, Carmin, Kristin, the chick at your old job . . . really?"

"You had no right to go through my things," he responded, before railing back about how I never let him have any privacy.

I was explosive, screaming and crying, working myself into such an emotional frenzy that I felt as if I were going to pass out. I couldn't calm myself at all. All I could do was listen to him assail my character for being a snoop. I sprawled out on the blue comforter, mouth agape, trying to think of how to respond. I suppose a lot of time passed while I was thinking, because he just hung up.

I called out sick to work and spent the rest of the day lamenting about what to do next. All I could think about was getting out of town and away from the situation. Seven hours later, when Bryce came home, I told him my plan.

"I am going to Norfolk for a speech in a couple of weeks. While I'm there, I'll probably hook up with an old high school friend."

"Okay, so, what are you trying to tell me?" Bryce asked. "Are you planning on sleeping with this dude to get back at me?"

"I'm just going to spend time with someone who actually wants to be with me—unlike you."

"I just feel a lot of pressure from you, Nika," Bryce said. "Ever since I moved in, all you talk about is getting married."

"I wasn't trying to pressure you," I snapped. "It's just we've been together so long and my career has been established, I just thought marriage was the next logical step."

"It's not. Something between us just isn't right, and it hasn't been for a while."

"What are you saying?" I asked. "You want out? Why not just leave instead of cheating on me?"

"I didn't want you to find out," Bryce replied. "I didn't mean to hurt you. You're my best friend. I'm sorry. I've just been unhappy."

I've been unhappy too, I thought, *but until now I never wanted to be with anyone but you.*

I remained numb and feeling unwanted until Bryan called just before I went to bed that night. His Southern drawl lulled me, as it had done nearly twenty years earlier. I was immediately drawn in, hanging on every word that came out of his mouth and traveled through the phone line to my ear. Curiously, I listened, waiting for him to reveal the reason he'd sought me out after all this time, but he didn't tip his hand.

My connection to him was instant from the second I answered my cell phone, so much so that the years between our last conversation and this one melted away. There was no awkwardness; there were no long pauses, no questions or answers that were off limits as we frenetically tried to bring each other up to speed on our lives. It was refreshing—exhilarating, even.

The only time I wasn't paying attention to what he was saying, I was wondering if Bryan was as attractive as he had once been. I wanted to know if his latte-colored skin was still smooth and flawless, as appetizing to look at as it had been pleasing to snuggle up next to during the one night we'd been so close together, we'd melded into one.

Our chemistry that night was combustible: it ignited in a flash, right after Bryan shut the door to our private room and wrapped his strapping arms around my waist. He wasted no time using his agile fingers to undo the clasp on the top of my ivory strapless dress, then nudged the zipper down just enough for the garment to fall onto the floor. Standing before him in my matching undergarments, I felt a rush of cold air across my shoulders, which the warmth of his chest quickly replaced. I extended my arms, letting every part of me intertwine with him. He delighted in my readiness to give myself to him and seized the moment, scooping me up and placing me atop a counter in the room.

He slowly inched my ivory lace boy-short panties down my smooth, waxed legs until they dangled around my ankles, just above my three-inch heels. Unsure of what he would do next, I awaited his every move. But he surprised me by simply scooting me forward until my body dangled on the edge and, moving his lips in, kissing my inner thighs. Keenly aware of what was coming next, I closed my eyes and delighted in every flick of his tongue, the gentle grazing of his slight mustache on my clit, and the warmth of his breath on my inner lips.

My low murmurs seemed to further excite him, and he began to explore every crevice between my legs with his mouth. He was so deep
inside me, I could see only the top of his head when I periodically glanced down. He kept himself buried there, lapping up my very essence, until he saw my legs trembling uncontrollably; that's when he took my hand, ushered me down so we were standing face-to-face, and let me sample what I tasted like to him.

Just before the fervor between us crossed over a threshold I'd never passed with anyone, I pulled back. I stood in front of him, trembling in rapture but unable to tell him or show him how much I wanted to continue. For a few seconds, he stood staring at me with his saucer-size eyes, willing me back, closer to him. But somehow I resisted, extending only my hand. He took it in his, and with his warm grip on top of mine, he slid my palm down his chest until I reached his manhood. From there, he took over, guiding me in how he liked to be touched so he could reach climax. It wasn't long before he did—I knew because I could feel his gratification drip down my hand.

But that was then and this is now, I thought, as we talked on the phone now, years after that night. *Now we are old enough to do what we feel like, without any judgment from others.* There was nothing to stop me from exploring Bryan, except for the physical distance between us and the fact that he was married—albeit in an open marriage, according to him.

Bryan and I exchanged text messages for the next few days, arranging a time, day and place to meet up. We decided we'd have to rendezvous at a location far from where either of us lived. Once we agreed, I booked an out of the way hotel and waited for time to pass.

I toiled for the next couple of weeks, trying to pretend I wasn't becoming increasingly more eager to see Bryan face-to-face, and on edge because the tension and fighting at home between Bryce and me were at volatile levels. We both dreaded waking up every day because a new argument would ensue within moments. Oddly, though, neither of us could walk away. We still loved each other despite the fighting. Perhaps, we also believed that one or both of us would get tired of the fighting and it would just stop. Then, we could go back to our relationship before all of Bryce's cheating and my bitterness ate away at us. However, we just continued what we termed Battledome day in and day out, trying to find a way to release the anger we both felt.

The only relief I had was knowing I had a speech to give in Norfolk, Virginia, about my book, *I Didn't Work This Hard Just to Get Married*, so I knew I'd be free from the ongoing drama for at least one night. Well, that and I was going to see Bryan. He and I had exchanged nothing but longing messages since we decided to get together. Yet, I still had to wonder if we were just trading fantasies.

What if the chemistry we had was gone and we have nothing to talk about in person? I thought. *Worse yet*

, what if the lust that has filled me for the past few weeks was only on my end? I would be left wanting Bryan while he simply drank his drink, shook my hand, and walked away.

When the day came, I popped out of bed, bounded to the shower, and sprinted to my car for the seven-hour drive to Old Dominion. I barely spoke to Bryce before I left the house, except to remind him of the time of my speech and to say I'd call him later.

My hands shook the entire drive down the New Jersey Turnpike and into Virginia. I was a nervous wreck, wondering if I should feel guilty for cheating on my boyfriend or if I should somehow verify what Bryan had told me about the state of his relationship with his wife. To work through my confusion, I stopped at the first rest station I saw and got myself a large cup of coffee.

Just then, my cell phone rang. It was Bryan, seemingly aware that I needed to hear the sound of his voice to stop me from turning around and heading home, skipping my event to avoid him. Bryan was hyper and as giddy as a child about laying eyes on me in a short while. His enthusiasm validated my yearnings, which had filled me with vivid fantasies that interrupted my sleep. For the first time in weeks, I was at ease, knowing the anticipation of seeing each other wasn't just on my end. My mind was free from the exasperating thoughts that had put me on edge, and I was able to motor to the Inner Harbor to deliver my speech without fretting over our visit again.

I delivered my brief remarks in front of a crowd of women in their forties in record time. I tried to focus on the Q&A session, but I found myself giving terse responses. I couldn't wait to get out of that restaurant so I could head over to meet Bryan.

Nearly forty-five more minutes passed before I could finally leave. By the time I pulled into a space at the Sheraton Norfolk Waterside Hotel, where I was staying and he was slated to meet me, I was back to being my confident self. I knew I looked good, I knew he wanted to see me, and I knew I couldn't wait to see him.

I sprang from the car the second I parked and sprinted to the front desk to get my card key. I pressed the UP button at the elevator at least a dozen times before it finally came. Dashing inside, I stood in the back of the mirrored car, clutching my overnight bag and using my free hand to make sure every hair was in place before I walked to my room. Finally, I
reached the sixth floor and tried to settle myself, because by then my heart was racing. I managed to get my fluctuating emotions under control by the

time I got to my room. Tranquil now, I slipped the card into the reader, waited for the green light, then flipped the door open.

A sheepish smile crept across my lips when I saw him standing in front of me, inside my room, just waiting. I immediately dropped my eyes to his feet, savoring every second as I worked my way up his body, examining every inch of him. He looked very much the same as I remembered: still burly, still fetching, and still irresistible. I knew I was in trouble.

"Can I have a hug?" he uttered, as he slunk over to me with his arms outstretched.

I didn't even answer. I just tiptoed forward until I could feel the heat radiating from his body.

Once in his solid grasp, I shuddered with pure glee, comfortable and turned on by him at the same time. The feeling unnerved me, but I didn't scurry away from him until the split second my lips grazed the side of his cheek.

"Let me put my bag down," I said, as I turned my back and tried to fight the urge to prowl over to him, push him down on the bed, and do anything that came to mind.

"You seem nervous," he responded, chuckling. "You don't have to be. I won't hurt you—that is, unless you like that kind of thing."

"I'm fine," I snapped back. "I just want to get settled, that's all."

"Okay," he snickered. "Well, while you're doing that, you might want to just look over at the window to your right. Those flowers are for you."

I brought my eyes up from my bag just enough to see the robust bouquet sitting a few feet from me.

"Thank you," I said, as I tried to resist squealing in delight. "They're beautiful. You really didn't have to."

"Well, I was hoping they'd inspire you to be nice to me," he quipped. "Do they?"

I didn't respond. I just sauntered over to the edge of the king-size bed and sat down. As soon as my buttocks landed on the fluffy white down comforter, he strolled over, positioning his body in between my partly open legs. He bent down slightly, kissing me on the lips, before placing one hand behind my head, drawing me closer so our kiss became more ardent.

I was spellbound, and there was no turning back. I submitted to him, letting him climb on top of me and peel away the layers of my clothing until we both lay there bare. From there everything flowed. He slipped inside me, forcing me to let out a soothing gasp of air. He seemed to fill me up with his length and width, providing me with more satisfaction than I had thought possible.

By the time we were completely worn out, it was the wee hours of the next morning. We remained strewn across the bed, still holding each other's hand, and simply drifted off to sleep. I couldn't stay that way, though; I kept opening my eyes, watching him slumber peacefully. I almost couldn't believe how our meeting had resulted in a mind-blowing crescendo of ardor that had led to a cherished evening I didn't want to end.

Soon, however, it was eight o'clock, time for him to head to work and for me to answer my phone, which had already rung twice in a row. I rolled over and answered it, even though I saw it was Bryce on the line.

"Hello," I whispered, while trying to sound as normal as possible.

"How was your night?" Bryce asked. "You see Bryan?"

"I did, and he's still here."

"Where? In your room? So, he stayed the night?"

"Yeah, he did," I responded. "Can we talk about this when I get home?"

Bryce didn't answer the question. He just abruptly hung up the phone.

Now you know what it feels like to be me, I thought. *For years I sat twiddling my thumbs at home while you were on the prowl for anyone who would spread it for you. It hurts for the shoe to be on the other foot, doesn't it?*

As I rose from the bed, Bryan emerged from the bathroom, fully dressed.

"Come here," he uttered, as he walked right up to me, pulling me in close to him.

I didn't get a chance to say anything before his mouth swallowed mine, his tongue probing deeply, forcing me to let out a delightful moan. We stayed locked together until our hands began fumbling with each other's clothes and we realized if we didn't part, neither of us would ever leave. As we peeled ourselves off each other, he placed three delicate pecks on my lips.

"I gotta go," he whispered. "But I would like to see you again."

Inside I bounded with glee, but I responded, "I'll let you know."

I sat for a moment, trying to contain my joy. However, my respite was short-lived. He called less than five minutes later, frantic.

"I paid the hotel bill on my credit card so I could get into the room while waiting for you. Can you go downstairs and switch it to your card so my wife doesn't find out?" said Bryan.

I immediately became nauseous, realizing he and his wife were probably not in an open marriage, the way he had described it to me.

How could I be so stupid? I thought. *I must've wanted to believe Bryan isn't with his wife anymore, that he wanted to be with me, that someone wants me and no one else, that I am someone's first choice. What the fuck is wrong with me? If I can't stand when Bryce treats me like the runner-up in his life sometimes, why would I put up with it from Bryan? Well, I need to just forget him. I'm not about to be his side piece.*

I shook off my dismay and rushed to the lobby to settle the bill so I was no longer of any concern to him. As I got back to the room, I slumped onto the bed and thought, *Oh shit, now I've taken the last step to pushing Bryce out the door. He'll never forgive me like I've forgiven him. I don't know if I want him to, but I didn't want to go out like this. Where was my head?*

I collected my bag and hustled out to my car to begin the tedious drive back to New Jersey. Every time I took a step, I felt the right side of my head pound. The pain got more and more intense, until it was so severe, I had to clench my jaw to stop myself from crying out.

Guilt is a motherfucker, isn't it? I thought. *It's kicking my butt right now. I'd better stop somewhere and get some aspirin, because I can't make it home like this.*

Tears began to run down my cheeks as I struggled to keep driving toward the nearest turnpike rest stop.

Whew, I thought, as I pulled into the parking lot of a service area just over the New Jersey border.

Hobbled by the stabbing pain in the side of my head, I stumbled into the convenience store and picked up a tube of Advil. My hands shook as I struggled to remove money from my pocket to pay for the pills. Finally, drugs in hand, I made it back to my car, flopped down in the seat, and swallowed three capsules straight away.

Come on, please work.

I waited about ten minutes, but the pain had subsided only slightly. I decided I had to fight through it and keep going if I was going to get back to my home before I was due at work.

I sped out of the rest area and got right back on the New Jersey Turnpike. I alternated between holding the wheel with both hands and pressing one firmly against the side of my head, pushing back against the nagging throbbing. Nothing worked.

Maybe if I could take my mind off this infernal pain, I'd feel better, I thought. *Perhaps I should call Bryce and talk things out with him now.*

I pushed the SPEAKER button on my cell phone as it lay in the center armrest and anxiously waited for him to pick up.

"Bryce," I shouted.

"Yeah, Nika, what's up?"

"I don't feel good," I uttered. "My head is killing me. It hurts worse than it ever has. I can barely focus."

"That's probably God punishing you for what you did."

"I know and I'm sorry," I said, wincing as the pain suddenly got worse.

"Did you take anything?" Bryce asked.

"I tried three Advil, but it's doing nothing at all."

"Where are you?"

"I'm almost home. I'm near exit thirteen. It's . . . it's just getting worse."

I didn't get the chance to say anything else. A dagger shot through my head, instantly blacking out my vision and mottling my hearing. I clasped the wheel tightly and tried to keep the car steady.

Oh shit, I thought. *I can't see. I can't see. What am I going to do?*

My heart pounded furiously as I debated whether to pull over or to try to continue going straight, even though I was able to see only the red brake lights of the car in front of me and shadowy images on either side of the vehicle.

I have to keep going, I thought. *I have to get home. I'm scared. I can't stop, because I don't know where the side of the road is, and I can't get out of this lane, because I can't see. Let's hope this guy in front of me is getting off soon. I'm going to have to stay behind him.*

I continued to drive straight ahead. I shook my head back and forth, irrationally hoping the motion would jar my vision back into focus.

Thankfully, I was able to get off at the next exit, which was mine. My vision returned slightly but was still distorted. Everything around me was covered in a bizarre haze. Despite all the illnesses I'd had, I had always maintained 20/20 vision. My sight was also the one sense I most feared losing.

I didn't get out of the car when I reached my parking lot. I just sat there, head resting on the wheel, trying to figure out what to do. I couldn't see well enough to call Bryce back to even tell him I was outside. As it turned out, I didn't have to at all. He came strolling out of the house and was next to the driver's-side window within minutes of my arrival.

"You okay?" asked Bryce, as he flung my door open and bent down at my side.

"No, I feel awful," I muttered. "I think I'm really sick."

"Well, I will help you inside so you can lie down, but I'm going to meet my dad. I'm taking him to dinner in the city for his birthday."

"Okay," I stammered, leaning my weight on him as we made our way up the front stairs to the townhouse.

I flopped down on the sofa, clutching a bottle of aspirin and the glass of water Bryce gave me, as I listened to him leave the house.

He hates me, I thought, *and I don't blame him. Maybe I deserve to be suffering right now.*

That was the last thought I had before I drifted off to sleep. When I awoke an hour and a half later, my vision had returned and the pain in my head was almost undetectable.

I can still make it to work, I thought, as I grabbed my sweater and slowly walked out of the house and back to my car.

My twenty-minute drive to the city seemed effortless. I could see and hear clearly. It was as if a weight had been lifted off me just by getting home and looking Bryce in the eye. However, within moments after I got to my office, I could feel that excruciating head pain return.

I should be fine now, I thought. *I have more aspirin in me than any one person should, and yet I can't seem to shake this pain for more than a couple of hours.*

I laid my head on my keyboard as I tried to gather myself at my desk. Quickly, though, the pain became debilitating again and I was unable to move. I could hear my coworker Mary calling out to me; I struggled to form an intelligible response and could not.

Mary sauntered over to me and said, "How are you feeling, honey? Are you okay?"

Once again, I tried to get anything out, but all I said was something she couldn't understand.

Mary laid her hand on the back of my neck and exclaimed, "You're burning up! You need to go to the hospital."

Her proclamation kicked off a flurry of activity. Our 6:00 PM producer raced to my side and asked whom he should notify about my
illness. Our remote production coordinator came over and began monitoring my pulse. The assignment-desk manager on duty called down to security to have an ambulance sent over. All I could do while this was going on was try not to burst into tears.

It took all of five minutes before two men wheeling an ambulance gurney were in my line of sight. They rushed over to my desk and immediately began attaching oxygen to me. I was helpless, at their mercy, unable to make any decisions about my care. Luckily, Mary didn't leave my side. She told them about my medication, then walked beside me as they loaded me into the ambulance downstairs.

Mary and I got to the emergency room within minutes. By that time, my temperature was already 104 degrees. I was aching all over, and all I wanted was to see Bryce.

"Have you been here before?" asked the admitting nurse.

"Yes."

"Can you spell your name for me?"

I used all the strength I had to fulfill her request, and, lo and behold, there I was, right in the computer system; that meant I didn't have to fill out any new forms. I could simply be wheeled into a room and wait for a doctor to figure out what was going on.

"We called Bryce," said Mary. "He's eating dinner with his dad but says he'll be here as soon as he can. Until he comes, I'm going to stay with you."

Mary and our manager on duty, Kim, sat by my bedside as I began to writhe in pain.

"She needs drugs!" Mary yelled at every nurse passing by. "The pain is too bad. She's suffering. When is someone coming?"

A nurse raced into the room and began hooking me up to an EKG machine. I could see the readout streaming from the machine as I lay there, but I couldn't read it. I knew it couldn't be normal, though, because I was starting to feel a bizarre sharp pain in my chest.

"Have you ever had an irregular heartbeat before?" asked the nurse.

"No. Why?" I asked.

"It seems like your fever may be causing one. Let me get a doctor in here as soon as possible."

As soon as she stepped out, I asked Mary, "Has anyone called Bryce again?"

"I'll call him right now, honey."

I lay there wondering if Bryce was even going to show up at the hospital, if he even cared if I lived or died.

"He says he and his dad are finishing up now; then they'll be here," said Mary, bursting back into the room, visibly annoyed. "I don't know what's taking him so long, but he's coming."

Mary had just finished her sentence when the nurse came in with a doctor to look at me. My temperature and heart rate were still soaring, so the doctor ordered me downstairs for a CT scan to try to determine what was going on. I didn't want to go alone, but what choice did I have? I waved good-bye to Mary and Kim and took the long trip down the sterile white hallway with a strange man who didn't bother to introduce himself.

"You're going to stay here," he said. "Someone will come out to get you in a bit."

He was right. Someone came out and wheeled me into radiology a few minutes later. It was a place I'd been often, so I followed the instructions and allowed another total stranger to see exactly what I was made of psychologically. Shortly afterward, another stranger picked me up and began wheeling me back to the emergency room.

Surely Bryce is here by now, I thought. *I've been gone for a while.*

I was wrong. Mary was still waiting for me in the ER, but not Bryce.

The doctor came in almost immediately. "The radiologist has looked at your scan, and we can't find anything, so we'd like to do a spinal tap," he said. "Someone will come in to explain the process to you before you give your consent."

"I can't stay for that," Mary said. "I hate needles."

I'm going to be alone when someone jams a giant needle in my spine, extracts fluid, and potentially leaves me paralyzed, I thought.

I was just about to break down, when Bryce sashayed through the door, carrying a bottle of wine.

"What's going on?" he asked.

"They want to do a spinal tap," I replied.

"Well, you're going to have to let them do it, baby girl. Are you okay?"

How dare you act like everything is fine after you took so long to come see me? I wondered. *I suppose you think I deserve to be punished for what I did with Bryan, huh? Well, maybe you should consider how many times you betrayed me and yet whenever you called I was right by your side without hesitation. Well, you're here now and that's all that matters, I guess.*

Relief washed over me and I said, "I'm okay now."

The doctor and his assistant came back in, carrying the anesthesia that was going to be used in the procedure. I quickly read over the paperwork and signed, giving them the right to use me as a human pincushion.

"Okay, you are going to need to remain completely still. This is going to hurt, so hold on to the bed if you need to," the assistant said.

I put both hands firmly on the side rail, took a deep breath, and braced myself for the assistant to stab me in the back. An explosive pain shot through me as she jabbed relentlessly, trying to find the right track to inject the drug. I could feel it oozing inside me and waited for relief, but it didn't come.

"Ms. Beamon, I think I missed the right area for the drug, so either I can inject you again or we can do the spinal tap without it."

"Do it without," I said, wiping away the long line of tears collecting on my face.

"Are you sure?" she asked.

"Just do it, damn it," I snapped. "Let's get this over with."

With that, the nurse inserted the spinal needle, then began extracting fluid. I wasn't sure how long I'd be able to remain still in the fetal position. I wanted to hop up and run screaming from the room, but somehow I held on until the procedure was done.

Bryce re-entered the room and sat by my side as I waited for the results. He and I didn't say much to each other, but just knowing he was there helped me to feel better.

An hour later, the doctor returned and said the spinal tap was inconclusive but he believed I was suffering from some sort of infection. He handed me some Vicodin and told me I was free to go home; the pain should pass in a couple of days.

Bryce drove me home and took diligent care of me, along with my mother. The only problem was, I wasn't getting any better. Five days in, when I couldn't get my head off the pillow or see clearly again, they'd both had enough. He scooped me up into his arms and carried me down the three flights of stairs in our townhouse to my car. He sped into the city to our primary care physician's office and told him, "I've never seen her like this. Something is really wrong."

I was stretched out on the examination table in room one, drifting in and out of consciousness as Dr. Thomas examined me. I desperately hoped he'd have a clue about what was going on. Finally he said, "Honestly, I have no idea what's wrong, but you've been getting progressively worse over the years, so it's time we get to the bottom of it."

"What do we do?" I mumbled. "Tell me whom to see, and I will go. Just help me. I'm getting sicker and sicker, and no one seems to want to do anything about it."

"I care," said Dr. Thomas. "The first person I want you to see is Dr. Levine. He's in the otolaryngology department at St. Luke's. He will examine your ears and your eyes to get to the root of your problems with your vision and hearing. Once I get his report, we will take the next step. I will also give you strong pain meds and an antibiotic, just in case you have an infection we haven't detected yet. It can't hurt."

Bryce grabbed my prescriptions while we waited to hear when I could see Dr. Levine. Moments later, we had an answer.

"Dr. Levine can see you in an hour, if you can get over there," Dr. Thomas said.

Neither I nor Bryce even answered. Bryce just wrapped his large arms around me, lifted me to my feet, and ushered me back to the car to make the ten-block drive over to the hospital.

"How are you, Ms. Beamon?" Dr. Levine said as he walked into the room, carrying a folder bearing my name. "I just got off the phone with Dr. Thomas, and he told me about what's been going on with you. Can you give me more details?"

I recounted how my vision suddenly went out on the highway, leaving me as blind as Stevie Wonder behind the wheel. I even joked that I used "the Force" to guide me home that day and was relieved when my sight suddenly returned. Then I told him how my joy faded when my vision blurred again hours later, after I arrived at work.

"Now my sight seems to come and go, when my fever gets high, and a sharp pain stabs me in the side of the head," I said.

"Can you see the chart over there on the wall?"

"Yes."

"Tell me which one of those faces, which represent a pain scale of one to ten, best describes your level of pain."

"It's about an eight," I said, cradling my head in my hands.

"Okay, please tilt your head back. I'm going to use this flexible laryngoscope to look into your nose to see what's going on."

The long black tube snaked through my right nostril, leaving searing pain in its wake. The only good part was, I no longer thought about the throbbing on the side of my head. I was actually anticipating the doctor's yanking the tube out and delivering good news: that he had found something to explain my deteriorating health.

"Well, other than some inflammation and a little mucus, everything looks clear," said Dr. Levine. "I think it's best if we get an MRI of your head and neck now to see if a clot or a tumor is blocking the blood supply to your brain."

What the fuck? I thought. *Now I have to go home and worry about dying in my sleep. Who says this to a person and doesn't even blink?*

"I think this will really give me a clearer picture of your condition," Dr. Levine continued.

I collected my referral form and headed back to the car for what seemed like the longest and quietest ride home Bryce and I had ever had. I reclined the seat fully so it was practically lying right on top of the backseat and tried to calm my brain. So many thoughts were flooding it.

Whatever this mystery illness is will render me an invalid before any of the doctors figure it out, I thought. *I'm deteriorating and I'm being brushed off like my ailment is trivial. It's not to me. If I can't see, how do I write? Writing is how I earn a living. Better yet, how do I take care of myself or live alone. I can't. No one cares about **any** of this.*

I just wanted quiet. I wanted my conscience to shut the hell up, honestly. After all, it was making me so nervous, I wanted to vomit.

I must've fainted, because when I came to, Bryce was on the passenger side of the car, ready to escort me back into the house.

Who the hell let me buy a townhouse? I thought, staring at the two flights of stairs leading to my front door. *This is some bull. I can barely get across the parking lot. How the heck am I supposed to get up those stairs?*

Bryce placed his arm under mine and leaned my side against his to give me support as we climbed the first five stairs, then the next.

Whew, I thought. *At least we made it to the front door.*

Bryce flung the door open, revealing the eight stairs leading up to my first floor.

"Fuck!" I shouted, looking at the obstacle before me.

"Just take your time," whispered Bryce. "I'm right here. I've got you."

Frustrated, I pushed his arm away and got down on all fours. I crawled up step by step, like a toddler learning to navigate stairs. It took me probably three times as long as it would've if I had just let Bryce help, but when I got to the top, I had a sense of accomplishment: even semi-deaf and visually impaired, I could do something for myself.

I crawled over to the love seat and perched myself on my knees, then used all of my remaining strength to pull myself up and tumble down onto the cushions. I was thoroughly exhausted, as if I'd run five miles. Sweating and worn out, I lay there while Bryce grabbed a tray table and set up my pain pills, my regular medication, water, and crackers. I was home. I was at peace. I stayed in that spot for two days, leaving it only to go to the bathroom, until it was time for my MRI.

It was far too early when I opened my eyes to get ready for Bryce to drive me to West Side Radiology in Midtown. Ordinarily I wouldn't have scheduled any appointment before 9:00 AM, but I wanted to get this done. Besides, by now, I needed to know if I'd ever return to my normal level of functioning, with perfect sight and hearing.

My mind felt blank as I walked inside the center and registered for the test. I wasn't scared, nervous, or anything—I was just ready. The techs were ready for me too. I waited barely ten minutes before they hustled me into the back to disrobe so they could shove me inside the MRI machine.

"If you're ready, Ms. Beamon, you can follow me." the technician said.

I shuffled behind her in my sock feet, slipping on what appeared to be freshly washed and buffed floors. Thankfully, I went just a few feet and entered a room on the right. An enormous white machine was there to greet me.

I placed my body flat against the slab and waited for the tech to place my head in a restraint. She strapped down my forehead, so I had almost no mobility; all I could do was look straight up.

"I'm going to tilt this mirror so you can see outside the machine," the technician said. "This should help with your feelings of claustrophobia."

How is a mirror going to help? I wondered. *I am going to be slid inside this giant machine with about two inches of clearance all around me, unable to even turn my head. This is going to suck no matter what.*

I could hear every high-pitched sound, gear shift, and squeal of the machine for the torturous minutes I spent inside it. It was maddening to think about what each hiss, beep, or grinding noise meant; was it actually reading something on my brain and neck?

I didn't learn until two days later that a hemangioma, or a benign tumor at the back of my sinuses, pressing on the base of my brain, might be to blame for my troubles.

As relieved as I was to know that guilt alone wasn't the source of my medical issues, Dr. Levine thought it best to do nothing about the bizarre growth inside my body, other than to watch it.

How is this a good plan? I wondered.

As soon as I left his office, I called Dr. Thomas for a referral to a neurologist. I knew I wasn't going to get any better until I became more proactive about my own health.

Chapter 10: Blackie

I'd become an old lady in a matter of months. I was unable to drive alone on a major highway because my doctors weren't certain I could keep my car on the road. It took round-the-clock care from my mom and Bryce for weeks before my vision and hearing returned fully, although no one knew what had caused my miraculous recovery. Still, my primary care physician, Dr. Thomas, cautioned me against getting behind the wheel without a driving buddy.

The revelation that I couldn't operate a car without a chaperone began to make me feel as if I were a step away from someone's taking away my keys because they feared I'd plow into a storefront after mistaking the gas for the brake, or mow down a crowd of people after hopping a curb because I was too ill or disoriented to stop the car.

I played along with my doctor for three months, but I was itching to get back on the road to continue my book tour. I decided one way to do it would be to disguise these trips as girls' weekends with my mother.

My mother was always up for an adventure, so when I called her to invite her to join me on a three-hour road trip from my home in New Jersey to Baltimore, so I could be a featured speaker during ladies' night at the Baltimore Book Festival, she didn't hesitate to consent. It was the first time since my father's illness and my temporary disability that I'd left town to do anything, let alone headline an event to promote my book *I Didn't Work This Hard Just to Get Married*.

My mother sat confidently in the passenger seat as I drove. I didn't mind doing all the driving; it was what I had wanted all along. I needed to know that I could do it, that I'd really recovered fully. I think my mother was wondering the same thing, although she never let on.

We arrived at Inner Harbor at least an hour and a half before I was due onstage. It was the earliest I'd ever gotten to an event.

My mother and I strolled into the luxury hotel the event promoter booked for me, and promptly checked in so we could get out of our driving clothes and into outfits more befitting an author and her mother. Our traveling clothes made us look like two lost, disheveled women, rather than anyone the literati would take seriously.

I carefully removed my brown, pink, and white halter dress from its bag and ironed it while my mother freshened up in the bathroom. When she finished in there, it was my turn to shower and flatiron my hair.

With my hair freshly pressed and my body smelling like vanilla and lavender, I was ready to exit the steamy bathroom, but I put on my deodorant reluctantly, because my armpits were on fire. The itching was almost unbearable. I scratched and scratched, until I realized there was blood underneath my fingernails.

Gross, I thought. *This is not the day for this.*

I splashed water on my pits and cautiously took a look at them in the mirror. The slices my nails had made through the skin exposed the pink, bloody flesh. Even more disturbing was the deep, dark color of my armpits. The pigment of my pits was bluish-purple and sagging like elephant skin, in complete contrast with the mahogany shade of the rest of my body. I dabbed the blood away with toilet tissue, thoroughly cleaning the wound. Once my armpits dried enough for me to delicately dab deodorant on them, I walked out of the bathroom as if nothing was wrong.

My bizarre affliction would've gone unnoticed if it weren't ninety degrees outside and I had chosen to wear a dress without sleeves. Seconds after I dropped my towel and stepped into my dress, my mother noticed my problem.

"What is wrong with your armpits?" she asked, grabbing my wrist and snatching my arm into the air. "They are as black as charcoal."

"I know," I snapped, lowering my arms. "I just noticed that in the bathroom. They've itched since I got really sick, but I didn't think it was a big deal."

"That's not normal," she exclaimed. "You need to get that checked out."

"I will when we get back," I said, unsure if I was actually telling her the truth. "Right now, we need to go. I'm onstage in forty-five minutes."

My mother and I walked the nearly two miles to the other side of Baltimore. I was amazed I made it, considering I was wearing big-girl shoes, which I call any heels over two inches, be they wedges or not. The uphill part of our journey was the worst; fatigue was getting the best of me when we hit flat land again. Years of relative inactivity had left me in woefully worse shape than my sixty-year-old mother, who had only one kidney and a rod in her leg. I tried not to let on whenever I took a break; I'd just slow down and point out landmarks or other seemingly interesting sights.

Finally, when I noticed several book vendors straight across the street from us, I said, "We made it!" The bustling area was filled with more book lovers than I'd been around in months; it was an author's paradise. The attendees' enthusiasm seemed to pump up my own energy levels, until I felt ready to walk some more.

My mother and I made our way to the authors' welcome center so I could check in. Instantly, I was face-to-face with famous scribes and the three young women who'd be participating in my panel: Andrea Lavinthal, Jessica Rozier, and Nicole Porter, who'd also written about the joys and pains of single life but whose books I hadn't read.

My mother and I walked to the nearby tented location where I'd be speaking.

A wine bar was set up in the back of the tent to provide free samples to the seventy-five or so people waiting to listen to us babble on about girl power. I considered snagging a glass for myself, to calm my nerves, but since all of my medication came with a big yellow sticker advising against alcohol, I stayed away and turned to the next-best soothing option, and my only vice since college: candy. It's a good thing I had something to calm me, because the moderator came over, introduced herself, and grilled the panelists for information.

"Can each of you tell me a little something about yourself and your book?" she said.

Shouldn't she have read our books and bios? I thought, as I spouted off the promotional copy about my book, rather than thinking of something new or interesting to say.

Then the moderator said something stunning: "After I introduce you, each of you will read an excerpt from your book. Afterward, I will open up the floor to questions."

What? I thought. *No one told me I had to read from my book. Hell*
, I don't even have a copy with me.

Panic-stricken, I sat onstage, wondering what I was going to do. I contemplated taking off my microphone, running over to the authors' tent, and grabbing a copy of my book. However, I decided against it.

They fucked this up, so it's going to be what it's going to be, I thought.

"Are you okay?" my mother mouthed from the audience.

I could only shake my head no. I didn't think she understood what I meant until she rose, approached the stage, and handed me a copy of my book, which she had tucked into her giant mommy purse.

"Here," she said. "I noticed all the other women on the panel had theirs, so I thought you'd need yours."

I cradled the book, silently thanking her, as she made her way back to her seat.

As the program got under way, I tuned out the other women, for the most part, as I tried to figure out what I was going to say about my own book. They seemed clear, organized, focused, while I knew I was flying blind. I feared I'd sound like a blithering idiot, until the moment the moderator turned to me.

"Well, unlike my colleagues, I'm not going to read something from my book. I'll just tell you about it and me," I said.

With that I began a rambling speech that often prompted laughter from the crowd. I'd hit my stride and wasn't worried anymore about how I sounded; I knew that I had the audience eating out of the palm of my hand. I focused squarely on my mother; her very presence settled me down. I felt like I was holding a private conversation with her, and that was all that truly mattered to me.

"For someone who said she didn't know what to say, Ms. Beamon sure said a lot," the moderator joked, taking the floor back from me.

After I fielded the majority of the questions from the crowd, the session ended.

"You are your father's daughter," my mother said, walking up to me as I took off my microphone and left the stage.

"What do you mean?" I asked.

"He has that gift, to talk to and charm a room," she continued. "This was the first time I saw that you have it too, but you do."

"Is that a compliment?" I quipped, reaching up and scratching my armpits.

"Would you stop scratching!" my mother shouted.

"I can't help it," I responded, as we walked over to the authors' autographing tent.

I was about to start another scratching fit when a middle-aged woman approached me with my book in her hand.

"Can I have a hug?" asked the woman.

I'm not that friendly, I thought, but I suppressed my inclination to shy away. I patted the woman gently on the top of her back, then quickly released her. *I hope that sufficed.*

"Can you sign my book?" she asked.

"Sure."

"Actually, it's not for me; it's for my daughter. This is the perfect book for her."

"Hopefully she'll find she can relate to one of the ladies in the book."

This brief exchange distracted me temporarily from the constant itching in my armpits, but once the woman was gone, it was in the forefront of my mind again. I gingerly scratched the raw skin periodically as my mother and I strolled back to our hotel. Once there, I cleaned my armpits again and applied deodorant and baby powder, hoping that would help me make it through dinner without any more irritation. It did.

My mother and I left Baltimore the next morning and headed straight to my friend's baby shower in southern New Jersey. The constant irritation of my armpits distracted me from the festivities. It served as a nagging reminder for me to call and make an appointment with a dermatologist as soon as I reached home.

I'd barely stepped in the door of my townhouse before I got on the line to Dr. Thomas. First, I asked him for a referral to a neurologist, something I'd neglected to get since my spontaneous recovery from my sight and hearing issues. Then I made sure to get a referral to the best dermatologist he knew.

"I know the perfect guy. Dr. Gupta used to be an internal medicine specialist but went into dermatology a few years ago. He may be just what we need to get to the bottom of things," said Dr. Thomas. "He's down by NYU, so it's a little out of your way, but I think it's worth it."

"I don't mind going out of my way if we finally get some real answers," I snapped.

"I told you I'd do my best, and I will keep trying," Dr. Thomas responded. "As for the neurologist, I'm going to give you the number of the chief of neurology at your regular hospital. He will have access to your MRI and all of your recent blood tests."

"Thank you," I replied. "I'm sorry for being short with you—I'm just on edge. It seems like there's always something."

As soon as we hung up, I called the two doctors whose names I got from Dr. Thomas to set up the appointments. Luckily, the dermatologist said he was free to see me in just a couple of days. It would be several days after that when I could get the neurologist to take a second look at my MRI.

On the day of my appointment with Dr. Gupta, I parked near Washington Square and strolled the five blocks to his office, nestled on the first floor of a swanky Greenwich Village building. I felt more like I was headed to a friend's apartment for tea than going to meet a stranger who would be probing me.

The door to unit 2B swung open, revealing an ultramodern office with a Lucite reception desk. Behind it were four private rooms on either side of the wall, each with a frosted-glass door and windows. It was also eerily silent. There was no Musak playing and no talking from the two other patients. The only sound was from the ringing phone.

I stood before the nearly expressionless receptionist, waiting for her to at least ask me why I was there.

"You must be Ms. Beamon," she finally said. "Dr. Gupta will see you now."

What? I thought. *I've never gotten in to see a doctor this quickly.*

"Please have a seat in the first waiting room, and he'll be right in," she continued.

I sat in the giant gray-leather reclining chair, swinging my feet as I nervously anticipated the doctor's arrival, but I didn't have to wait long.

"Nika, what brings you here today?" Dr. Gupta asked when he entered.

"A weird problem, actually," I said. "My armpits have turned black. I mean, I know I'm black, but my armpits are really crayon-black. They itch a lot and cause me to scratch them until they bleed."

"I think I know what's going on," said Dr. Gupta.

"Are you serious?"

"I read on your form that you take metformin. Is that for insulin resistance or PCOS?"

"Both, actually," I said. "You are the first doctor not to think I was diabetic."

"I've seen this before," he responded. "If you don't mind, please slip your shirt off and put on this gown. I want to take a look at your armpits. I may also have to look at the inside of your thighs. You don't have to take your pants off; just open the top and slide them down a bit." He left the room while I happily obliged, anxious to learn what he thought was wrong with me. Partially naked and cold, I couldn't wait for Dr. Gupta to come back in and examine me.

"Okay, let's take a look," he said, wheeling his chair first to the right of me, then to the left, peeking at my armpits.

Afterward, he rolled toward my feet and looked up at the inner part of both of my thighs. "It looks like you have a condition called acanthosis nigricans."

"What's that?"

"It could be just a skin condition that causes these dark, thick, velvety layers of skin in places across your body," he said. "But it could also be the sign of something greater, like cancer, so I want to do a biopsy; that just means I will take a small sample of skin from one of your armpits and your thigh to test it."

Cancer? I thought. *I would never have guessed that.*

I sat motionless as I felt him snip skin from both my thighs and my armpits. The wounds stung but didn't bleed too much.

"You will get a call from me with the results in three days at the most," said Dr. Gupta. "Do you have any questions?"

"Yes, a bizarre one," I said, hesitating to finish my thought. "Is it possible that this 'condition' is related to something that happened to me a month and a half ago?"

"Tell me about it," Dr. Gupta said.

"I was driving down the road, and suddenly I felt sharp pains in my head. A few minutes later my vision went out, my hearing became distorted, and I was in so much pain I couldn't think. I went to the hospital, and my blood pressure was, like, 180 over 110, and my temperature was 104. I had a spinal tap, and it showed nothing. In an MRI, the doctors found a hemangioma in the back of my sinuses, pressing on my brain, but they really never came up with a real reason why that happened to me."

"Well, without seeing the records, it would be hard for me to say what actually happened. But a spike in your insulin could cause a TIA, or transient ischemic attack, or a stroke. I think that sounds more likely to be what happened. Has it happened before?"

"The same thing happened again a few days after the first incident, but it seems to have passed now."

"I would say you should have a neurologist check your MRI and your endocrinologist check your insulin levels, just to be sure. I believe all of your problems may be related."

"You're the first doctor to say that," I said.

"Don't stop looking for the cause until you find a doctor who gives you an answer," he said as he stood, preparing to leave the room. "If there's anything else I can do, please let me know. In the meantime, go see the neurologist and endocrinologist. I will call you in a few days, hopefully with good news."

I bounded out of Dr. Gupta's office finally feeling heard and understood by a doctor for the first time in more than a decade.

I can't believe it, I thought. *There really could be an explanation for all of my strange medical problems.*

I bolted to my car to begin the drive home, determined to look up the condition Dr. Gupta had just described to me.

I've been suffering all this time, and there could've been a solution. It's clear that no one other than Dr. Gupta has been looking at the big picture, I thought. *I need to Google everything they've said that's wrong with me, including non-alcoholic fatty liver disease, gastroesophageal reflux disease, polyps, hemangioma, and acanthosis nigricans to see if any one condition explains it all. I also need to make sure these drugs they've been pumping me full of aren't doing more harm than good.*

I fired up my Compaq Presario the second I got home to begin my search for every ailment that seemed even vaguely related to my odd collection of symptoms. I found everything from horrific terminal illnesses to mild conditions that could be easily cured. I was flooded with information, some of it confusing. Yet, despite it all, I finally felt empowered, like I was taking my own health seriously now and not just depending on others to clue me in to what was going on with my own body.

Perhaps I shouldn't do this, I thought. *I could become one of those hypochondriacs who believe every illness affects them or who run to the doctor for something as small as a splinter, thinking it's going to turn into an infection that will kill them.*

Despite the crazy thoughts running rampant in my head, I continued to scour the web until I had a comprehensive list of ailments that resembled mine. I then prepared myself to go head-to-head with my new collection of doctors until one of them could tell me the nature of my defects.

Chapter 11: I Can See What You're Thinking

An aging, white-haired man with a gruff voice entered the examination room, grumbling to himself. He didn't extend his hand to introduce himself or to put me at ease. He walked right over to his desk with what I presumed to be my file, plopped down into his chair, and swung around so his back was to me.

"Why are you still back there?" he shouted, noticing me sitting on the exam table in the back of the room. "I need to talk to you before I look at you."

"Oh, okay," I responded, momentarily intimidated by the abrasive nature.

He continued thumbing through images and files on his computer screen for several minutes before he said another word to me. Then he turned his chair around and spoke: "Well, what brings you in here today?"

"Um, I'm Nika Beamon—"

"I know that by looking at your file," he interrupted.

"Anyway," I continued, "I'm here because I've been to several other doctors, who haven't been able to pinpoint the source of my medical problems. The last doctor I saw told me to bring you my MRI showing the hemangioma at the back of my sinus, my recent blood tests, and his report about my skin condition to see if you could determine what's going on. He also mentioned he believes an incident I had on the highway that prompted me to see all these doctors could've been the result of a TIA, or a series of them."

"I don't know what doctor you're talking about, but I looked at all of your reports, and I wouldn't say you had a stroke. You're young and otherwise healthy, so he could've been grasping at straws," he said.

"That may be true, Dr. Marshall, but *something* happened, because I couldn't see or hear on two separate occasions, which doesn't make sense. I may have a host of problems, but I've never had any issues with my sight or hearing before."

"Okay, okay," he said. "Tell me what happened when you first lost your vision."

I recounted the entire highway story to Dr. Marshall, who sat with his head bowed, furiously scratching notes on a piece of paper. When I finished, he looked up and scolded me like a grandfather talking to his granddaughter.

"Listen to me," said Dr. Marshall. "If that ever happens to you again, pull off the road. You should never keep driving. You were a danger to yourself and everyone else on the road."

"I understand that," I responded, my voice quivering. "I was scared and just trying to get home without getting mowed down by other drivers on the turnpike. God willing, nothing like that will happen again. That's why I'm here."

"I'll have to look at you to figure out if that will be the case," Dr. Marshall sniped.

He wheeled himself over to me as I prepped myself for his exam by removing my shoes. As soon as I lifted my head, he began whipping off a series of neurological questions to test my brain function. Then he was on to physical tests of my motion skills. He ran a reflex hammer over the bottom of my feet, then whacked my knee with it to see if I had any nervous-system damage. He also tapped a tuning fork on my knee and asked me if I could feel the vibration. After that, he did a finger-to-nose test, a ankle-to-tibia test, and a resistance test. This last test was similar to something bullies used to do in elementary school: he smacked my hands or pushed against them to see how much force I could exert back.

I seemed to pass all of his tests with flying colors, and he concluded, "If you had a stroke, it was a minor one, because you don't appear to have any residual effects. I won't speak in certainties without other tests. If you had a stroke, given your age, this could be a sign of more to come." He walked back over to his desk. "TIAs in people under forty-five can mean you have a heart or vascular problem or are suffering from a chronic infection or persistent inflammation. The spinal tap didn't show a chronic infection, although Dr. Thomas's tests did find some sort of infection. You have evidence of some chronic inflammation, based on your liver tests, so I'd like you to see a cardiologist to rule out a heart or artery defect."

Another doctor? I thought. *This is becoming exhausting.*

"Do you remember what the nurse said your blood pressure was, Ms. Beamon?" Dr. Marshall asked.

"She didn't take it," I responded, while putting my shoes back on.

Dr. Marshall opened the exam-room door and bellowed down the hall to his nurse, "Please take Ms. Beamon's vitals so I can write them on the chart. This should've been done before I came in to see her."

Well, at least this dude isn't a jackass just to me, I thought. *He chastises his staff in front of patients.*

The nurse flew into the room with her stethoscope swinging in the air around her neck. She dashed over to me, clearly flustered, and jammed a paper thermometer into my mouth. It gave me a paper cut as I quickly tried to lift my tongue.

"One hundred," said the nurse. "That's a low-grade fever. Do you have them often?"

"Yes, I run spontaneous fevers sometimes," I responded. "Sometimes I'll be fine but then one will come out of the blue."

"Make sure you tell Dr. Marshall about it."

Isn't that your job? I thought, as she rolled up my shirtsleeve and fastened the Velcro on a blood pressure cuff.

I stared at the diagram of a brain on the wall in front of me while the machine inflated and deflated on my scrawny little arm.

"One fifty over ninety," she said. "How do you feel?"

"Fine. Why?" I asked, as she hustled out of the room in search of Dr. Marshall.

For the first time all day, he came into the room with a look of concern on his face. That, of course, raised my anxiety.

"What's wrong?"

"I'm going to take your blood pressure again myself," Dr. Marshall said, glaring at his nurse in disgust.

He snatched the blood pressure cuff off the top of the machine, then yanked my arm back toward him. He placed his stethoscope in the crease of my arm and listened to my pulse without the machine. He then double-checked his results by using the machine.

"Are you light-headed?" he asked. "Do you have a history of high blood pressure? I didn't see that in your file."

"No," I said, with a newfound sense of angst. "The last time my blood pressure was high was the day I lost my sight, was rushed to the hospital, and had a spinal tap."

"High blood pressure, even intermittent, could cause a stroke," he said abruptly. "At this level, you could have another one at any time."

Are you fucking kidding me? I wondered. *Is he going to do something to help me?*

"What do I do?" I asked.

"I'm going to give you a blood pressure medicine called verapamil and a baby aspirin. They should prevent you from having a stroke," he said, dashing from the room. It was the fastest I'd seen him move during my entire visit.

He came back in with a Dixie cup full of water and a pale purple pill in his hand, along with a peach one.

"Take these and then lie down," he barked. "I will **be** back in a few minutes to check on you."

Dr. Marshall called out to his nurse a second later, "Dorothy, get Ms. Beamon's primary care physician on the line. I need to talk with him."

A few minutes later, his nurse shouted, "Dr. Thomas is on the line."

Dr. Marshall didn't respond to her. He snatched the receiver off the phone on the wall and began explaining what was going on with me to Dr. Thomas. When he hung up, he abruptly turned to me and said, "Dr. Thomas wants you to go see him in a couple of days, before you go back to work."

"I was planning to go tomorrow," I said.

"No. I want you to fill the prescription for more blood pressure pills, get thirty-milligram baby aspirin, and relax for a couple of days. You should take your blood pressure every few hours. If it doesn't go back down to an acceptable range in a day or two, go back to the emergency room."

"Okay," I muttered.

I came in for him to fix me, and I'm leaving more damaged than before, I thought.

"Can I leave?" I asked, so thoroughly through with this doctor, I wanted to run out of the office.

"Not until your blood pressure drops a little bit," he responded, shutting off the lights in the room and instructing me to lie back down.

I lay there in the dark, contemplating what to do next while wondering if my body was a ticking time bomb.

This is ridiculous, I thought. *More pills! I need to find a doctor who doesn't think drugs are the solution to everything.*

After Dr. Marshall checked me two more times, I was free to leave. I motored as fast as my legs would carry me to the elevator and repeatedly pushed the DOWN button. I knew it wouldn't make the elevator come any faster, but I still hoped it would. When it did arrive, it was packed. There was no way I'd let that stop me from getting out of that office. For once, despite seeing two or three morbidly obese people jammed in the elevator with me and eight others, I didn't worry about the weight limit. I smushed my body into the car next to a man I didn't know and rode face-to-face with him.

Once the elevator stopped on the ground floor, I dashed out of the building and headed straight for Duane Reade to fill my new prescriptions. As I waited, I made an appointment with the cardiologist.

I hope and pray this guy can finally figure out what's been going wrong and fix it, I thought.

Chapter 12: Say "Ah"

Opening my mouth wide and saying "ah" was an action I'd gotten really good at by the time I went to see Dr. Rosenbaum, my cardiologist. I'd googled him and checked out his rating on ZocDoc.com before confirming my appointment. Most of the patients who commented online said he was helpful, kind, and knowledgeable—three traits I was really looking for at that point. He was also in demand. It took me nearly two months to get to see him.

As I lay on a plain black table in my underwear, Dr. Rosenbaum wheeled a large table filled with monitors and screens I'd never seen before over to me. It looked like something at NASA or in some sort of research lab. There were tons of wires hanging off the machine, and it made a host of weird sounds, even without anyone or anything connected to it.

"First, I'm going to ask you a few questions about your medical history," Dr. Rosenbaun said. "Afterward, I'm going to connect you to an electrocardiogram machine. It will monitor the electrical activity in your heart through these twelve leads, which I will attach to you. I'll be looking for rhythm abnormalities, so it's important that you stay relaxed and still."

"I've had an EKG before, but I thank you for explaining things to me," I said, as I stretched out and waited to be hooked up like some sort of lab rat.

I lay there listening to my heart beat, worried that it would skip a beat or that the doctor would detect some unknown defect, but I didn't hear anything odd or see any bizarre jumps in the waveform printing out on the piece of paper coming from the machine.

Dr. Rosenbaum ripped off the paper and examined the results at a table right across from me. He didn't immediately say anything, and that concerned me. Then he mumbled, "You can get dressed now and meet me in my office."

I hurried to get back into my clothes so I could hear what he'd uncovered.

"I looked at your file and see you take Actos," Dr. Rosenbaum said.

"Yes, I take it for PCOS," I said.

"I'm sure your doctor told you that Actos has been linked to congestive heart failure."

"No, she didn't tell me that," I responded, trying to ascertain whether he was telling me this was my problem.

"Well, she should have. You should be on a water pill. I'm going to give you a prescription for one."

Another drug? I thought. *I can't catch a break.*

"I also think you should have a transesophageal echocardiogram," Dr. Rosenbaum continued.

"Why? What's that?" I asked. "Did you see something wrong on my EKG?"

"No, there's no need to panic," he replied. "It will give me a clearer image of your heart, especially the arteries leading to and from it, so I can see if there are any blood clots that could explain your suspected TIAs."

"Okay," I said, breathing a small sigh of relief.

"I must tell you, it is a major procedure, so you will need to check in to the hospital and undergo general anesthesia; that means someone will have to pick you up and bring you home," Dr. Rosenbaum continued.

"Oh, I'm single. I'm going to have to find someone to bring me home, then," I said, becoming uneasy as it hit me that this was going to be my first major doctor's appointment without Bryce by my side.

Bryce had moved away just a few weeks earlier. He'd gone on a trip to the Gulf Coast to visit a childhood friend after another one of our epic fights, and he'd had an epiphany. When he got back, he immediately announced that he hated his job and was quitting. That didn't shock me, but his next announcement did. He said he'd already found a position in Virginia and would be moving there in a couple of weeks. He didn't ask me to go, didn't say he'd start looking for a job to bring him back, and never discussed a plan for me to visit. He didn't say he was leaving for good, but in my soul, I knew he was, and I knew his omissions were his way of telling me that.

I thought about begging him to stay, not to leave me to face my illness alone, but I thought it would be fruitless. Plus, I wanted him to stay with me because he wanted to, and I sensed that wasn't the case. I did the only thing I thought I could: I tried to be understanding. I helped him pack up his car, hugged him, and watched him drive away from me.

I hadn't spoken to him for a week and a half when Dr. Rosenbaum told me about the latest test I needed to get. I considered calling Bryce as soon as I found out, but I waited until I was on my way home, alone in the car, to call. I tried him three times in row and got nothing but voice mail. I was starting to feel like a stalker, when he finally called me back.

"How are you?" I said, bracing myself for what he might say next.

"I'm fine, and you?" Bryce responded coldly.

"I'm okay, except I haven't heard from you in a while," I sniped. "You been busy, or is there something you want to tell me?"

"Like what?"

"How about why you haven't called?"

"I have been busy getting settled here," Bryce replied.

"Is that it?"

"No, it's not."

"I need to ask you: Do you still want to date me?" I asked, petrified about his possible response.

"I think I want to be single."

His words hung in the air as I fought back the urge to collapse into tears. "Okay," I said. "I always told you to just be honest with me, and you have been."

"I love you, but all we do is fight all the time, and I can't take it anymore. I think it's better that we are not together."

"I understand," I said, even though I didn't.

I believed he and I could make it through anything. After all, he didn't bolt whenever I was sick, and I didn't leave just because he cheated on me.

"You okay?" Bryce asked, with genuine concern in his voice.

"I will be."

"You know I will always care about you," Bryce continued. "I will always be there for you."

"How?" I asked. "You're not here for me now."

"What's that mean? I'm here, talking to you. Is something else going on that I should know about?"

"No, no," I said, rolling my eyes. "I'll be all right. I should let you go."

What am I going to do without him? I wondered as I hung up the phone.

Alone in my bedroom, I was afraid of being in my house by myself for the first time since I had moved in. It felt so empty and so lonely now that I knew Bryce was never coming home. Everything I looked at and touched reminded me of him. Even the sheets I was lying on conjured up memories of us laughing in bed, rolling around together, or images of him sleeping peacefully by my side.

What if I get really sick again? I wondered. *Who is*

going to help me now? Who is going to love me the way that I am? I can't believe he's really gone. I can't believe he gave up on me—on us.

I picked up the phone to call my girlfriend to **ask** her to take me to my medical procedure but then hesitated, thinking for a moment that she might not to be able to help me because she was caring for an infant on her own. I knew I couldn't take any more rejection. I was already down, embarrassed that at my age I didn't have anyone other than this friend and my parents to come and get me. I knew my mother was scheduled to be at work while my father was out trying to get his cheesecake business off the ground, so I didn't want to be a burden to them. Diane was my last resort.

Diane hadn't held a full-time job since her mother had been diagnosed with bone cancer, more than two years earlier. Less than a year after her mom passed, she gave birth to her first child, a son. She was left to be a single mom, one who didn't have any parents, because her father had died just a few years before her mother.

Diane had a key to my townhouse and was a frequent guest there throughout her pregnancy. I could tell she was lonely, in need of a friend, after her son's father didn't seem all that interested in her sonogram and her doctor's visits. I relished the opportunity to be there, to see a life from the very beginning. Birthing a child was an experience I'd begun to think I'd never have, so Diane's pregnancy was the closest I'd get to it. The best part was, Diane seemed to enjoy sharing all of her private moments with her fetus with me. She let me see every image, told me about the heartbeat, kicking, everything.

She'll come, I thought, as the phone rang for the fourth time. *She won't let me down. We've always been there for each other; this will be no different.*

"He left me," I said when she answered, barely able to get the words out.

"I know he moved away," Diane said.

"No, he *left* me," I exclaimed.

"What happened?"

"He said he doesn't want me anymore. Nearly a decade later, and he's just throwing me away. All the things he's done to me, all the other women, and I never gave up on him."

"I know, honey, but he's not you," Diane said. Her words hurt me like a slap in the face. "It's his loss. You were good to him—better than he deserved. He should've been grateful to be with you."

"What am I going to do without him?" I asked, hoping she really did have an answer. "He's always been there for me when I've been sick. Now what?"

"Is something wrong right now?" Diane asked. "It seems like there's something you aren't telling me."

"I need to go in for another procedure," I replied. "That's why I called him; I was going to ask him to come back and help me, but he was so cold and distant, I never even bothered."

"So he doesn't even know?" she asked.

"No. Why should I have said anything? He doesn't care about me anymore, if he ever really did."

"Well, *I* care, honey," Diane said, in the most comforting voice she could muster. "If you need me, I'm there."

"I need someone to pick me up from a procedure I have to have at NYU," I said hesitantly.

"Of course I'll be there, but tell me what's going on."

"I'm having a transesophageal echocardiogram. My doctor says he needs a better look at my heart to try to figure out why I had those strokes."

"Well, I will be there to get you, so don't worry about that," she said. "I wish I could take away your heartache too, but I can't. I am sorry. I know you loved him."

"I know I have to get over this, but I never loved anyone the way I love him."

"I know that. Someday he will know what he's missing by not having you."

"He says he wants to be friends. He says he'll always be there for me. I just don't think I can. Am I wrong for not wanting him in my life at all if I'm not with him?"

"Don't focus on him right now," she said. "You need to take care of yourself and try to get healthy. Pray over the rest. God will heal your heart."

"From your lips to God's ear," I said, before hanging up the phone.

I cried myself to sleep that night and every one afterward, until my hospital appointment arrived a week later.

I got to the hospital that morning by myself and checked in at the admissions desk. I considered calling Bryce to tell him where I was and what I was having done, just to see if he still cared about me at all. I didn't, though. I just cradled my cell phone in my hand and prayed he would somehow know to reach out to me this one time so I could be calm.But he didn't get my psychic message.

"Ms. Beamon, you can come into the back now to meet with the anesthesiologist," the nurse said.

I walked down yet another barren hallway in yet another hospital to meet with yet another doctor.

I'm starting to feel like an inmate on the way to the lethal-injection chamber, I thought. *Everyone seems reluctant to make eye contact with me, like they know some horrible secret about my fate that I don't and guilt is overwhelming them.*

I strapped on my wristband and double-checked my information on it, then signed the form affirming I knew what procedure I was having. I'd read horror stories about people who failed to read the paperwork and doctors cut off the wrong limb, took out the wrong organ, or performed the wrong procedure.

I had just finished triple-checking everything when the anesthesiologist came into the room and began explaining that he'd be putting me under with propofol.

That drug? Really? I thought. *Before Michael Jackson died, I had never heard of propofol. Now every time I step foot in a hospital, someone mentions using it.*

"I am going to weigh you and take your height

measurement so I can calculate how much of the drug you need for this procedure," the anesthesiologist said. "Just so you know, propofol is a very safe drug when used by a skilled professional."

Yeah, that's what Michael thought, and look at where that got him, I thought. *I'm just praying I wake up.*

"You just need to sign these consent forms, and then we can get started," the anesthesiologist continued.

Of course—you need me to absolve you just in case you kill me or turn me into a vegetable, I thought.

I lay there flat on my back, hooked up to an IV drip for a few moments, before I slipped into nothingness. I wasn't asleep, but I certainly wasn't awake. I had no idea the doctor had begun the procedure, nor did I know when it was finished. I simply opened my eyes, glanced up at the clock, and noticed two hours had passed.

"Can you hear me, Ms. Beamon?" Dr. Rosenbaum asked. "We're all done. We're going to wheel you to the recovery room. In about an hour, the nurse will allow you to go home if your ride is here. You may feel a little groggy for the rest of the day, so please go home and sleep it off."

I drifted in and out of alertness for I don't know how long, before the nurse tapped me and told me Diane was waiting to drive me home. I lumbered to my feet and put my clothes on slowly. It took me an inordinate amount of time to get dressed.

I took tiny steps toward the exit, making sure I was steady enough on my feet to make it there without falling. My vision was distorted, and I felt completely out of sorts, but somehow I kept it together long enough to reach Diane. Thankfully, she had her son's stroller with her, and I used it to steady myself as we made our way down to her SUV, which was parked on the street.

Ugh, this again, I thought, as I stared out the car window at the stairs leading to my front door. *I've got to move.*

Diane collapsed her son's stroller and stuck him in the Baby Björn on the front of her body. He dangled there as she walked up the stairs and used her key to open the front door. She went in ahead of me and got her son settled into a car seat on the floor before coming back to help me inside. I took small, tentative steps across the parking lot and over to the stairs. Then, as I had done before, I crawled up to my first level.

I plopped myself down on my love seat. Fortuitously, I had worn my Reebok track suit, which was comfortable enough for me to stretch out in without feeling cumbersome. I draped a quilt my Grandma Nettie had made across me. I wasn't there more than ten minutes before I drifted off to sleep.

When I woke up, Diane's son was standing over me with his binkie in his mouth. He was staring in my face, making soft, curious sounds. I thought if he had been able to talk, he would've asked me how I felt. Still, he somehow understood I wasn't well, because he stretched out his tiny hand and began stroking my hair. After a few minutes of that, he leaned his little face against mine, removed his binkie, and gave me a soft kiss. I was still horribly dizzy, nauseous, and weak, but his touch instantly took away my discomfort.

I spent the rest of the night in the same spot, waking up intermittently to see Diane's son watching me to make sure I was okay. I struggled to feign a smile for him, and he noticed. He cocked his head to the side and smiled back, then went **back to playing** with his toys.

The next morning when I arose, the residual effects of the drugs were gone but the toll that my constant cycle of doctor visits had taken on my psyche caused me to question my mortality.

I tried to hide it in front of Diane, but the feeling haunted me.

How long can my body endure all the invasions by doctors? I wondered. *It's draining me in every way, physically, emotionally, spiritually and financially. It would be easier for me and everyone who has spent years worrying about me if I just succumb to this illness. At least we wouldn't be on edge anymore waiting to see what was going to happen next.*

My thoughts subsided only after the doctor called to tell me my heart and the arteries surrounding it appeared normal.

How could that be? I thought. *I feel a real pain in my chest all the time now.*

Diane and her son left me the next day, and I headed back to work as if nothing was wrong. I plastered a smile on my face every day, trying to hide the aching in my heart. I longed to know whether Bryce would ever check on me. I was also desperate to know whether I would ever be healthy enough to be on my own for the rest of my life if he really didn't ever come back.

Chapter 13: Humpty Dumpty

I stopped worrying about my own mortality when I got the news that my grandmother, the only one I had left, had died.

"Good morning, baby girl," my mother said, with deep sadness in her voice. "Grandma is gone."

"What?" I asked, as I rose from my desk in search of a quiet place to continue talking to her on my cell phone. I paused just inside the stairwell in the rear of my office and continued: "I'm so sorry. I can't believe it."

"I know, it's hard," she said, trying to comfort me. "I went over to the nursing home with Aunt Lola after I got the call. She died in her sleep. She looked so peaceful."

I used to joke with my grandmother that she'd outlive all of her grandkids. I and the other offspring of her children seemed to be plagued with a variety of bizarre ailments as we got older, while Grandma Nettie was as strong as an ox and very rarely sick. My recent health challenges had made me oddly jealous of her; I thought I'd never see the ripe old age of ninety-five, as she had. Grandma Nettie felt differently. When my parents and I broke the news to her that I was chronically ill and not getting better, she simply said, "From the day we are all born, we're dying, so no sense in feeling sorry for yourself. Be thankful. Every day is a gift for each of us."

I thought, *Yeah, but some people have an easier time enjoying their gifts, because they are healthy, wealthy, and/or wise. I am losing ground on all counts. I'm hemorrhaging money paying for medical bills, the doctors are playing catch-up with my illnesses, and I feel as if I'm losing my mind.*

Grandma Nettie couldn't hear what I was thinking, but she sensed it and chimed in, "At least you know something is wrong with you, so there is still a chance they can fix it. Have faith. With God, everything is possible. If not, it's his will. You can still make the most of the time you have been given."

Pretty wise, I thought, especially from a woman with only a fourth-grade education.

I knew my grandmother had given me sound advice, but it was becoming increasingly harder just to carry on when my health was wavering from day to day. I was starting to believe my doctors wouldn't ever be able to put Humpty Dumpty back together again. I had begun referring to myself as the nursery rhyme character years earlier, when my body had first begun falling apart. The nickname seemed fitting because no matter how many procedures, surgeries, or tests I had, I was never whole again—a fact that often tested my faith. My daily prayers seemed to go unanswered, and I wasn't convinced that God was listening or had a desire to send a miracle my way. But when I really began to feel hopeless, I thought of my grandmother's words and they offered me a measure of comfort.

Who is going to lift me up when I am down now? I wondered when I learned she had died. I couldn't sleep that night, but I wasn't up crying either—not because I wasn't sad or because I wasn't immediately feeling her absence, but because every time I thought about Grandma Nettie, I had to smile, realizing how she dominated my memories, including those of my first home, 1303 Hicks Street.

It was a modest brick house with a white wrought-iron railing located in the middle of the Bronx. In hindsight, the house itself was nothing special; however, the fact that I shared it with Grandma Nettie, my brother Randy, Aunt Johnnie, Grandpa Ernest, Uncle Buck, and five of my cousins made it home. It was also the place where Grandma Nettie gave me my foundation. Some of our family dinners—and I don't just mean the ten of us—were so big that relatives poured out of every door and stood against the walls with plates, and children huddled in every corner. After all, how could family gatherings be small for the matriarch of the Brown family, which consisted of her sixteen brothers and sisters, their children and grandchildren, and scores of nieces, nephews, and cousins?

Grandma Nettie taught me selflessness at 1303 Hicks Street. "Out of a little bit, we must divide," she'd say. She shared her home, her money, and her time with any and all who asked for it, whether that meant serving in the choir and on the usher board at Beulah Baptist Church for decades, paying for the funerals of relatives who didn't have insurance, or donating 10 percent of her Social Security checks to charity.

Not long after my grandfather died, in 1978, my grandmother lost her home, and she and her sister were forced to move into a small, two-bedroom apartment on Corsa Avenue in the Bronx. My brother and I, as well as all of the other cousins who grew up with us, were all back home with our respective parents full-time. That's when Grandma Nettie reverted to being what a grandmother was intended to be: the person with whom I spent summers and occasional weekends.

Grandma Nettie might not have been there every day anymore, but her impact on my life was still mighty. I remember her sitting me down after my first fight and telling me to "fear no man," to stand up for myself and not let anyone run over me. She seemed to have a phrase designed to give me a guideline for living an upright life no matter what the situation.

She said, "Mind, now" whenever I did or said something she found disrespectful. One of my favorites, "Tell the truth and shame the devil," meant I should be as honest as possible, even if it was painful, because the alternative would lead me to even greater sins. Then there was "God is good all the time"; that taught me it's critical to have faith even in the face of adversity. It was an expression I clung to as I reflected on losing her.

For me, my second mother was gone, and I couldn't even begin to process the flood of emotions that overtook me that first night. I could see her face when I shut my eyes, and could visualize every inch of her four-foot-eleven frame.

The more I thought about Grandma Nettie, the more I noticed how much I'd become like her. I inherited her determination and independence. She didn't give up after having her first child at fourteen, leaving a dysfunctional marriage, and moving to New York for a better life. Even though it was rough working as a maid in Queens in the frigid cold—so cold her spit froze before it hit the ground and her legs felt like blocks of ice because women didn't wear pants back then—she kept going, sending what little money she made home to South Carolina to help support her young children. Decades later, she had never stopped learning and growing, and had made huge strides for a sharecropper's daughter. She adjusted to cable TV, call waiting, using a microwave, and anything else we threw at her. *If she could conquer all that*, I thought as I sat in silence on my couch, *I can get through her death and beat my medical problems too; it's what she would want.*

"I sent out an email asking for photos of Momma and for someone to deliver the eulogy at the funeral, but no one has responded. I also need a good picture of your grandmother," my mother said when I called her the next day.

"No one offered to do the eulogy?" I asked, disappointed. "Well, if nothing else, I have a great picture of Grandma—that one of us on the boat in Virginia that hangs on the wall in my house. I will take it down and scan it tonight and will email it to you tomorrow."

"Thanks," my mother said, sounding at least mildly relieved that one thing was off her plate. "I'm going to finish writing up her obituary tonight. Can I email it to you tomorrow to look it over?"

"Of course," I replied. "And if you can't find someone to deliver the eulogy, I'll do it."

"Are you sure?" my mother asked, seemingly shocked by my offer. "I know this is hard for you."

"It is, but I can't believe no one else will do it."

I'm one of the youngest grandchildren. I'm dumbfounded that none of those old-ass people volunteered to speak about the woman who gave and sacrificed so much for so many of them, I thought. *When Grandma Nettie was alive, I helped pay for her home care, bought her items to help her take a shower and get around, drove her to doctor's appointments, and visited her in the nursing home when she couldn't live alone anymore. Very few of them stepped up then, and they still can't do it now, even when she's gone. Disgusting!*

I really didn't think I could deliver the eulogy at first; that is, until I was done with my marathon evening filled with recollections of her. The words flowed out of me onto the paper before me, and in no time, I had an entire speech. Although I suspected jotting my thoughts down was far easier than getting them out in front of a room full of relatives, I wasn't overly concerned about stage fright—I was more worried that my temper would get the best of me.

But when I entered Beulah Baptist Church on West 130th Street in Harlem, I had nothing but peace in my heart. I wanted to remain calm and deliver my tribute to my grandmother in a fitting manner. When it was time, I strolled past the open casket containing the shell of the woman I once loved so much and rose into the pulpit. Standing in the spot where she used to look out, belting

"Sign Me Up for the Christian Jubilee," I spoke clearly, succinctly, and without a wobble in my voice.

I looked out at the generations that country girl had spawned and thought how pleased she'd have been to see everyone together again. But I also knew she would have been disappointed that some, maybe even a large portion, had disregarded the lessons she taught. As for me, I was energized, feeling that I was finally embracing the faith and hope she tried to give me about my illness and life in general.

I stepped down from my perch and silently vowed to move forward, to gather all the tools necessary to put my life back together again. I was struck by the thought that perhaps I needed one doctor, like the one I watched regularly on the medical drama *House*, to diagnose me correctly so I could finally be healed.

I know House isn't a real person; he's a TV character, I thought. *But at least on the show he never gives up on a patient, no matter how difficult the case, until he figures out what's wrong with them. How come I've never had a doctor that committed to treating me?*

Chapter 14: The Lineup

For countless hours, I searched on my computer for a doctor specializing in diagnosing difficult cases, but I was chasing my tail. Defeated, I gave up and went back to what had become my regular routine. Every other week, I was at one doctor or another. If it wasn't the endocrinologist, it was the gastroenterologist, the immunologist, or my primary care physician. Keeping track of all my doctors made me feel like a baseball manager overseeing a major-league team lineup: *Up next, Dr. Thomas. In third position, we have Dr. Marshall.* It was a mind-bending puzzle of people, places, times, and dates. Add to that the upwards of eight pills I was swallowing each day without seemingly deriving any physical benefits, and I was starting to decline mentally.

I didn't recognize my depression until my sleep habits became more erratic. Nightmarish scenarios—like my impending death or disfigurement from some experimental surgery—began to plague me. My sleep deprivation progressed into melancholy thoughts of regaining control over my life by taking the same pills meant to sustain me to end my suffering permanently.

Fear of dying wasn't what stopped me from ending my life; it was an overwhelming sense of unpreparedness that gave me pause. I didn't want my family to be stuck with my financial burdens, like my mortgage or car payments, so I came up with the brilliant idea of buying more life insurance. What I didn't anticipate was that I'd have to pass a medical certification, which, of course, I couldn't. Time and time again, I was turned down. I was denied the right to buy additional coverage because, as the letters said, I was too ill.

Isn't insurance designed for those who are ill or dying? I wondered, as I read the letters.

The denials were the latest blow to my already-delicate psyche. I had been deemed unsuitable to purchase long-term disability from my job, because of my preexisting condition.

I was handcuffed, unable to die with the dignity of knowing I'd be debt free, and unable to live in peace because it was increasingly harder to get out of bed every day. The main motivation I had for rising and going to work was the medical benefits that being gainfully employed afforded me, as well as the meager life insurance I had already been able to secure.

The days dragged on as my depression deepened and triggered sudden crying fits. I would have to scamper off to the bathroom to find a stall for privacy while I attempted to get my emotions under control. I'd dry my eyes and shuffle back to my desk, trying to give no sign of the turmoil within. Some days it was all I could do to make it to my departure time of six o'clock so I could get into my car, race home, close the door, and collapse on the sofa in a ball.

I was starting to get used to my constant despair when I got a notice from my insurance company that sent me into an abyss of emotional despondency I'd never known before. It read: *Ms. Beamon—this is your quarterly statement of activity. You've spent $14,000 this quarter on medical bills. Here is the breakdown.* I didn't even look at the itemized portion; I just skipped to the bottom, which read: *Please be advised that there is a cap on your medical plan. At your current rate, you will exceed it in the next ten years.*

That's good to know, since I don't plan on living beyond fifty anyway, I told myself. *I mean, what am I supposed to do? Die before that time comes, or risk being bankrupted by medical bills?*

I felt helpless, the most vulnerable I had been since illness had begun to redefine my life. Yet I didn't know how powerless I could be until the phone rang a few months later. It was my father.

"Hey, Neeki," he said, trying to sound upbeat, though it was obvious he was not. "Mom's in the hospital."

"Is she okay?" I asked. I had a gut feeling the answer was no.

"No. She had a stroke," he replied.

I wanted to drop the phone, dart out the door, and head straight to my mommy's side, but I was paralyzed.

"The doctor says she's okay, but she's going to have to stay there for a couple days," my father continued. "You can go by tomorrow."

"Oh, so it's not that bad, then?"

"Well, she does have some damage. The right side of her face is drooping, and her speech is a bit slurred."

What? I thought. *My mother has always been there to take care of me when I was sick; she's always been strong. She's very rarely sick, and now this.*

I guess I hadn't said anything out loud for a few moments, because my father asked, "Are you okay, baby girl?"

"Yeah, I'm just going to talk to my boss to let him know I'll be here only a half day tomorrow, so I can go and see Mom," I replied, before hanging up the phone.

I wasn't sure how I was feeling as I got in my car and drove to the tip of Manhattan to see my mother. I was numb. The only thing I was sure about was that I wanted to be there for her, to nurse her back to health. I was no longer thinking of my own plight.

I tentatively entered my mother's hospital room as soon as visiting hours allowed. In an instant, I realized I was totally unprepared for what I saw. She was sitting in the middle of the bed, with her head facing away from me. When she turned in my direction, I could see her mouth hanging to the side, exposing her bottom teeth and causing her to drool. Her eyelid was sagging so low on the right side that the veins inside it and her eyeball were exposed more than normal.

"Hey there," I said, trying to pretend I didn't notice she was disfigured.

"Hi," she mumbled.

"How are you feeling?" I asked.

"I'm okay," she replied, then slurred a few other words I didn't understand.

I nodded and smiled, pretending I understood her so she wasn't self-conscious.

"You ready to go?" I joked. "The doctor says I can take you home if you're up to it."

"I am," she replied, keeping her responses terse so she wouldn't say anything she could mess up.

I sat by her side for half an hour, watching the toughest woman I knew in her weakest state. I didn't push her to talk. Her presence was enough for me. I just helped her gather her things, slowly, so I could drive her home. I had an impulse to take her to my house and tuck her away in my guest room so I could spend as many hours with her as possible, but I knew trying to lock her away wasn't going to change anything. The only thing that would help would be for me to get her well so we could spend more time together and create more memories.

Over the next few weeks, my mother's partial facial paralysis cleared up and her speech returned to normal. Along with the physical changes, her spirits lifted and she opened up about what happened the morning she fell ill. She candidly discussed how she ignored the warning signs of a stroke, from her persistent, piercing headache to a twitching in her cheeks. She also revealed that she was prediabetic and that this condition, combined with her high blood pressure, could have played a role in her stroke.

Just like me, I thought. *It sounds like some of the things ailing me are the same things that caused her stroke. Perhaps there's a genetic connection between what's going on with me and what happened to her.*

I ran this notion past my gastroenterologist. He was intrigued by
the idea but didn't seem all that interested in pursuing it. Rather, he set an appointment for me to come back for another follow-up exam. I agreed but vowed to push the issue when I saw him face-to-face.

Chapter 15: Do You Feel What I Feel?

"I have your results right here, Nika," my gastroenterologist, Dr. Ramdehal, said. "Your esophagus is inflamed, and it looks like you're developing another hiatal hernia. The long and short of it is that it appears you are right back to where you were seven years ago, before you had the laparoscopic Nissen flundoplication, the procedure to fix all of this."

"Why is that?" I asked. "I thought the surgery was supposed to take care of those problems for good."

"It made things better, but nothing is permanent," he said.

"Obviously," I snapped. "So what now?"

"You could have surgery again to tighten the stomach wrap and fix the hernia again. Then I can put you on Nexium to hopefully reduce the inflammation."

"That's it? More of the same?"

"It's the best I can do. I do think you need to figure out what's really going on with you," Dr. Ramdehal continued. "I know you've been trying to get to the bottom of it and haven't been successful."

Thanks for the pep talk, I thought. *I came to you, a doctor, to get answers—not to find them myself—but it seems the only time I ever make progress with my ailments is when I demand that doctors look high and low for information. Well, there's no more time to waste; I am not going to continue to be sliced up and pieced back together like the bride of Frankenstein.*

My head was spinning, and my stomach wasn't far behind. I was overcome by a wave of nausea that made me gag.

"Are you feeling okay?" Dr. Ramdehal asked.

"I think I'm having a bad reaction to the anesthesia from the endoscopy."

"Here," he said, handing me a piece of chewing gum. "This should help settle your stomach."

I sat in Dr. Ramdehal's office and looked around at the pictures of his wife and children, wondering whether, if any of them were sick like me, he would be so flip and nonchalant about helping them find a cure.

"How are you doing?" Dr. Ramdehal asked, sticking his head into the room.

"I'm okay."

"Well, let me check you out before you go," he continued.

Dr. Ramdehal touched my forehead to get an unscientific read on whether I had a fever. He then ran his hand down my neck to check my lymph nodes.

"Has this been swollen for a while?" he queried, pressing on the right side of my neck.

"It's been like that for about a month," I responded. "Why?"

"And it's been this sensitive to touch the whole time? It really hurts, doesn't it?"

"Yes, it does," I said, jerking my neck away from his hand.

"Let me call your primary care physician and have a quick chat with him."

This isn't good, I thought, reflecting on the last time a doctor had called Dr. Thomas in the middle of an appointment.

I buried my face in my hands, trying to settle myself as I waited for Dr. Ramdehal to come back into his office.

"Nika, I spoke to Dr. Thomas, and he and I agree that at this stage you should probably go to see an infectious-disease specialist. Something is causing your lymph nodes to swell. We suspect that same thing may be behind the inflammation of your esophagus and liver; it could be an infection of some sort."

"Okay, well, give me the number for a doctor, and I will call to make an appointment."

"No need," he interjected. "My assistant called, and Dr. Cornell can see you tomorrow."

I tossed and turned all night, not because of nervousness, but out of anticipation. I was one step closer to actually finding the underlying source to all my problems. I was so looking forward to my visit, I woke up before my alarm sounded. I flew out of the house and into the city, reaching Dr. Cornell's office in about thirty minutes.

"So, Dr. Ramdehal says you're a bit of a medical mystery," said Dr. Cornell, a petite woman with an uncomfortable smile. "Well, I like mysteries."

"Okay," I replied, wondering if she was really going to be able to help me, when so many before her had failed.

We spent nearly an hour going over my medical history, symptoms, and complaints as she plugged them into some computer program she didn't explain.

"Surprisingly, based on your answers and the test results I've seen, you don't seem to have a common illness."

Tell me something I don't know, I thought.

"I figured you had an autoimmune condition like sarcoidosis, which is chronic inflammation that can cause nodules to form in various
 organs; Graves' disease, which can cause an enlarged thyroid and trigger an irregular heartbeat and muscle weakness; multiple sclerosis, which affects the nervous system; or another disease, like sickle cell anemia, which is closely associated with African Americans, but you don't seem to have any of those," she said.

Really? Don't you think other doctors thought the same thing? I wondered. When is someone going to think outside the box, instead of looking at my surface to diagnose me?

"Looking at everything I've seen, I think you may have something like Kikuchi disease, a rare lymph node disorder; systematic lupus erythematosus, chronic inflammation throughout your whole body; or something even rarer."

"How do we figure out if you're right and which, if any of these, may be the culprit?"

"I'd like to run some very specific blood tests and get a CT scan done."

Dr. Cornell yelled out of her office door for her assistant to call my health care provider for a preapproval for the CT scan.

"While she's doing that, let's head into the exam room so I can check you out."

I hopped up on the table and waited to get yet another once-over from a complete stranger. At least this time Dr. Cornell didn't ask me to go au naturel. She informed me she just wanted to do a basic exam of my glands, blood pressure, and heart sounds.

She didn't get far into her exam before she stopped abruptly.

"Does this hurt?" she asked, after feeling my right lymph node.

"Yes, a lot," I said, jerking my face away from her hand, just as I had with Dr, Ramdehal.

"It's really swollen," she said, continuing to touch it, more gently this time. She slid her hand over to the left side and added, "This side is swollen too, but it's a bit better."

"They're constantly like this," I said.

"I can see why Dr. Ramdehal wanted me to see you right away. Swollen glands can be the sign of an infection or something far worse," said Dr. Cornell, jotting down notes on my chart. "Come back into my office. I think you should go see a colleague of mine right now."

I trailed behind her, a bit taken aback by the urgency in her voice. I'd barely taken a seat when Dr. Cornell's assistant rushed into the room to tell us that my health care provider refused to authorize the CT scan.

"That's okay," said Dr. Cornell. "Please get Ms. Beamon set up for an X-ray of her head and neck and pick up the referral slip I just printed."

Dr. Cornell turned back to me and said, "I'd like you to go see Dr. Biggs, a head and neck specialist. Are you free right now? I'd like you to go see him as soon as possible."

"Okay," I responded. "Is there a reason it has to be so soon?"

She didn't answer my question. Instead, she picked up the phone and began dialing.

"Dr. Biggs, Dr. Cornell here. I'm sitting here with a new patient of mine, Ms. Beamon. She has swollen lymph nodes on both sides of her neck, but her most recent blood tests reveal no sign of infection. I suspect something **else** is going on. Would you be able to take a look at her today and give me your opinion?"

As soon as she hung up, Dr. Cornell spun around and said, "Dr. Biggs can see you as soon as you can get to his office."

My head was spinning. I was trying to shake off any ominous thoughts that were creeping into my head, when Dr. Cornell interrupted me.

"Ms. Beamon, I think the best thing for you to do would be to get your X-rays first, then head to Dr. Biggs's office."

All I could say was "All right" as I gathered my things. I slipped my arms back into my jacket, collected my forms, and trudged the four blocks to the X-ray facility, which was coincidentally in the same building as Dr. Biggs's office.

The X-rays took about twenty minutes to complete, so I hoped they wouldn't interfere with my seeing Dr. Biggs. By that point, I was anxious to find out what he had to say. A few minutes after I arrived at his office, I learned just what his take was on my condition.

"It's nice to meet you, Ms. Beamon," said Dr. Biggs. "How are you feeling?"

"I'm okay, thanks," I replied.

"I hear you've been having a bit of a problem," he said, picking up a small light to begin his exam. "How tender are your lymph nodes?" he asked, while pressing on the right one so firmly my toes curled and it took every ounce of my effort not to scream out in pain.

"It really hurts," I replied, swatting his hand away.

Dr. Biggs lowered his hands and told me to head into his office. I was stunned by the abrupt end to his exam, until he settled into his chair and began to speak.

"So, how is Tuesday for you?" he asked.

"For what?"

"For surgery," he responded, seemingly confused by my question. "I need to remove that lymph node right away to biopsy it."

"A biopsy, as in a cancer test?" I queried.

"Yes, I thought Dr. Cornell told you she suspected lymphoma."

She didn't tell me anything, I thought. *I knew it was bad, just because of her urgency, but I didn't think about cancer.*

The shocked look on my face seemed to be enough to give Dr. Biggs pause and change his bedside manner from chilly to compassionate. He apologized profusely for springing the diagnosis on me, then took the time to explain the details of the surgery. When I appeared somewhat reassured, he asked, "Can you get an EKG by Monday?"

"I don't know," I mumbled, still dazed by the developments.

"I'll call your primary care physician to see if he can do it for you today."

Dr. Biggs immediately picked up his phone and dialed Dr. Thomas, quickly bringing him up to speed on my need for an EKG and the surgery I was now scheduled to have in just four days. I couldn't hear Dr. Thomas's response, but when Dr. Biggs hung up, he turned to me and told me to go straight to Dr. Thomas's office from there.

"Before you leave today, my assistant will bring you an envelope with all of the surgery information, including the location, time, and prep advice. It will also contain a prescription for Vicodin. You should fill that before surgery, because you will want it on hand when you get home.

Forty-five short minutes after meeting Dr. Biggs, I had agreed to put my life in his hands—the hands of a man whose first name I learned only when I read my prescription.

Chapter 16: Call Me Froggy

Shivering in a paper-thin gown in an oversize reclining chair in the presurgical room at the hospital, I was unsure if it was really chilly or if my nerves were getting the best of me. I tried not to think about the cold by reading fluff stories in *InStyle*, *People*, and *Us Weekly* magazines while waiting for the anesthesiologist to come and knock me out. I was actually looking forward to being unconscious so I could stop obsessing about the fact that the doctor was about to cut so close to my carotid artery.

"Are you cold, Ms. Beamon?" asked a male nurse sitting across from me, reading the newspaper.

"A little," I replied, rubbing both my arms to generate warmth.

The nurse didn't say anything; he just rose from his chair, walked over to what appeared to be a microwave, and pulled out a blanket. He carried it over to me and laid it on my lap.

"Wow, that's warm," I said.

"Yeah, we have a machine that heats them up now," he said in a
heavy Hispanic accent.

"I got heated blankets another time I was in the hospital, but they weren't this toasty," I replied, snuggling underneath the cover and relaxing while I continued my wait. I had just become comfortable enough to drift off to sleep, when an anesthesiologist came over and introduced himself.

"Which side is Dr. Biggs operating on today?" he asked.

"The right side, I believe," I answered, wondering if he truly didn't know the answer or if this was some sort of quiz to see if I had all of my faculties. "The left side is swollen too."

"Well, my form says the right, so let's go with that," he responded in an annoyingly chipper voice. "I am going to draw on the right side to indicate the incision site."

"Okay," I said, turning so he could reach it easily.

"Now I am going to put in the IV lines. We will use them to inject anesthesia once you are in the operating room."

I stuck out my left arm so he could insert the port into my hand. The initial sting of the needle insertion bothered me no more than a mosquito bite. It was the tape placed on top to hold the line in place that irritated me. My skin immediately started to itch, tempting me to yank the line out, but I resisted. I settled back into my chair so I could doze off again.

A few seconds later, someone else entered the room.

"I'm Michelle, and I'll be your anesthesiologist."

Why do I need two anesthesiologists? I thought.

"I will be in the OR with you, so I need you to read these forms and sign them," she continued.

"A different dude was just over here," I said irritably. "He claimed he was my anesthesiologist."

"He is, and so am I. We perform different functions," she replied.

Of course you do, I thought. *Doctors find new ways all the time to cost patients more money, don't they?*

I scribbled my name on the papers—admittedly without reading them thoroughly—then flopped back down on my pillow. At that point all I wanted was for all of the doctors to go away so I could have a moment of solace.

I closed my eyes and mumbled a silent prayer, asking God not to ensure my survival but rather to limit my pain and that of my family, regardless of the outcome. I prayed often, but now I took extra time to be thankful my doctors had caught my swollen lymph nodes before it was too late, and for having the courage to at least attempt surgery to save my life. I had no sooner finished uttering "amen," when I felt someone tapping on my foot.

"Ms. Beamon, are you done with your health care proxy?" said a random nurse.

"I am," I said, feeling around the side of the chair for the magazine that I'd jammed the form inside. I pulled it out and mulled over whether I'd done the right thing by leaving Bryce as my secondary contact after my father. Part of me felt I should swap out Bryce's name and place the name of my new boyfriend, Thomas, in that space, but I had reservations that Thomas would carry out my wishes.

Thomas and I met at work, although we didn't cross paths there often. The few times we initially ran into each other, things didn't go well. He was brash, as am I, so we constantly butted heads—that is, until our mutual friend, Monica, invited us both to dinner one night. It was the first time we'd had a pleasant conversation.

In the weeks following, Thomas and I chatted more often, but usually on a casual level. Then one day he passed by my desk and completely caught me off guard.

He glanced down at my thirty-day pill case, a birthday gift from my friend Kiada, and said, "Can I ask you a question?" He sat down on the edge of my desk and waited for me to speak.

"Okay, what's the question?" I snapped, looking up from my computer.

"Why do you take all those pills?"

"Do you really want to know?"

"I wouldn't have asked if I didn't," he replied. "Are you okay?"

"I don't know what to say, really. The short answer is, I have a chronic illness the doctors are trying to sort out, so I take pills **for everything from my stomach to my liver to my blood pressure.** You name it, I have a pill in this case for it."

Thomas paused, seemingly trying to process what I had just said, then asked, "Are the drugs helping you?"

"They're supposed to be," I replied.

I wondered why he cared and why he had stopped his day just to figure out what was going on with me, but I didn't ask him.

"What's next?" Thomas asked. "Will you have to take these pills forever? I mean, will you ever get better?"

"Well, I don't know if I will ever be 'normal.' One doctor told me my liver could fail and I'd need a transplant. Others have said I could stay this way forever. I've had a few close calls, and I have some days where I feel just fine. I really don't know if I will ever be healthy or not need drugs."

"I'm sorry you are going through this," Thomas said, with a melancholy look on his face. "If there's anything I can do, let me know."

"Thank you," I responded, feeling guilty that I had previously thought he was a jerk.

That one conversation spawned a succession of talks at work and several dinners over the next year or so. Thomas became a constant "ear"
and companion to me, easing me through my split with Bryce.

We both resisted getting physically entangled until we decided to take a weekend trip to Boston to attend a Red Sox game. Sleeping in the same
bed wasn't a problem the first night. It was the second night that changed everything. Just holding each other made it abundantly clear to both of us that our feelings extended beyond friendship.

After a few months passed I told Thomas about my "do not resuscitate" request and my desire not to be preserved by any artificial means should I get too sick to survive on my own. He didn't agree with my choices, but he had told me he'd honor them. Still, I couldn't help but be skeptical about what would really happen when I couldn't speak for myself.

This was my first go-round with Thomas, I thought. *I trust him with my heart, but my life is something entirely different.*

The other nagging thought I had was that Bryce had been by my side for ten years, through all of my hospitalizations and procedures, and he'd always done exactly what I asked. Despite our breakup, Bryce and I weren't estranged for long. He began calling to ask how I was feeling. Our talks soon branched out into other topics including work, family and friends. I even told him about my growing connection to Thomas. Before I noticed, we were talking multiple times a week. We'd developed a friendship, or at least a complicated relationship that resembled one.

I should leave Bryce on the form, I thought. *He may not want to be with me but he still **cares** about my health and well-being.*

I knew if the doctors called, he would answer and there'd be no question he'd follow the health care proxy the way I wanted.

I set aside my reservations about not adding Thomas to the form and handed it over to the nurse so she could witness my choices. She gave me a copy of the paper, which I promptly tucked back in my magazine, before closing my eyes once again.

Fuck, I can't get a moment of peace, I thought, as I heard someone faintly calling my name.

"Neeki, it's Dad," my father said.

I opened my eyes and saw my father standing over me, wearing his signature cowboy hat. He **had** a nervous smile on his face, the same one he always had when he visited me in a hospital. He looked at me, rubbing my legs to comfort himself more than me. He stayed by my side, making clumsy conversation, until Dr. Biggs walked in.

"My only concern is that your right lymph node is extremely close to your carotid artery. The proximity means the surgery might take longer than expected, because we don't want to nick it at all," Dr. Biggs said. "I am confident, though, that I can get it out whole and possibly eliminate your need for radiation, if it's in fact cancerous."

I waited for my father to say something, but he didn't. For once, he didn't give the doctor a hard time. Our silence seemed to perplex Dr. Biggs, so he asked us, "Do you have any questions?"

"I guess not," I responded, looking up at my dad for guidance.

"I will try to make the scar as small as possible," he continued. "There is always a chance that it will be a keloid."

"I don't think it will," I replied. "I've got a collection of other scars, and none of them have become keloids."

Once the Q&A was over, I was wheeled wide awake into the operating room. I thought I was all set to go under the knife, until the nurse placed her hand on my shoulder.

"Is that a bra?" she asked.

"Yeah," I said. "No one told me to take it off."

"That's okay; we will take it off here."

"Well, it's one of my favorites, and it was expensive, so I'd love to keep it."

"Believe me, I understand," said the nurse. "Do you think you can slide it off?"

It sounded easy enough to take off the bra like I used to do it in gym. I slid one arm out of the loop, then lifted my torso up so the nurse could shimmy it underneath me to the other side of my body. When it got to my left side, we realized there was a slight problem: the IV was preventing me from getting my arm completely out of the strap. The nurse removed the bra from my shoulder and tossed it to the top of the IV post; the doctor joked this was something he wasn't prepared to see. Ignoring him, a second nurse lifted up the IV post so the bra could fall down the pole to the floor. Once it hit the ground, the nurses picked it up, stuck it into a specimen bag, and taped it to my stomach. While I was distracted by watching all this, one of the anesthesiologists got down to the business of administering the solution that knocked me out a few seconds later.

The sound of deep moaning woke me out of a sound slumber. I pried my eyes open to find the source of the grating noise and locked eyes with a man with a mask of gauze on his face. The bandages were so large, he almost looked like he was trying to construct a mummy costume.

What the hell happened to him? I wondered.

As quickly as the thought came to me, it faded, replaced by my awareness of the throbbing coming from my own huge bandage. The wrap on my neck was so tight I could barely turn my head, and even swallowing was irritating.

"How are you doing, Neeki?" my father asked as he entered the recovery room. He was walking gingerly so the heels on his cowboy boots didn't disturb the two other patients, who had not yet emerged from their drug-induced sleep.

I opened my mouth to reply to him and heard a raspy, low, unrecognizable voice come out. I sounded kind of like Froggy from *The Little Rascals*.

"I'm ready," I uttered, trying to talk as little as possible.

I think my father knew that, because he said nothing else to me the entire ride home. He let me sleep, waking me just in time for me to walk up the stairs to my townhome. I must've used all the energy I had doing so, because shortly after I slipped off my shoes, I passed out on the love seat.

Thomas's voice woke me up several hours later.

"Hey, honey, how are you?" he asked, placing a gentle kiss on my forehead.

I adjusted in the chair until I was sitting upright so I could project as much sound as possible.

"I feel okay," I said, forcing a smile.

Thomas's blue eyes appeared to well up with tears as he stared at me. I could tell seeing me in pain hurt him, even made him feel helpless. He was by far the most sensitive guy I'd ever dated. His vulnerability, among other things, was what had made me question whether we should convert our yearlong friendship into a romantic relationship, and whether he could be the kind of man to stand beside me as I battled my chronic illness.

I resisted falling in love with him because I knew it was just a matter of time before some medical crisis would show me whether caring for me would be hard for him and might ultimately drive him away. We'd only spent nine months as a couple before I had the lymph node surgery and he had to decide whether to step up or step out of my life.

Now, as I lay on the sofa hours after my surgery, trying to shake off my grogginess, Thomas asked, "Can I get you anything?"

"I don't think so," I said, as I rolled back onto my side to take another quick nap.

Maybe I underestimated you, I thought staring at Thomas. *I doubted your commitment to me yet here you are waiting on me. I was sure that seeing my debilating condition in action would make you run. Instead you are looking at me with love in your eyes. I hope that never changes, no matter how sick I get.*

By the time I awoke again, about an hour later, my father was standing beside me. "Is it okay if I get ready to head home?" he asked. "I want to try to beat the traffic."

"Sure," I said, looking over at Thomas, wondering if he could truly feed me, drug me, and change my bandages.

As my father left my house, Thomas extended his arm and placed it under mine, bracing me as I made my way upstairs to the bedroom. He helped me change my clothes and slip under the covers, then went back downstairs to get a tray table to hold my medication, bottled water, a thermometer, and crackers for me to snack on. He snuggled up next to me and held me as I drifted off.

Two hours into my slumber, an excruciating pain jolted me awake. It shot through my jaw, down my neck, and through my collarbone. I tried to lift myself up so I could drink some water and take a Vicodin, but I couldn't get my head off the pillow. The aching was so intense, it rendered me speechless. I swung my arm, pounding the pillow in between Thomas and me until he woke up.

"What's wrong, honey?" he asked.

I didn't say anything. I just kept slapping the pillow, hoping he'd pick up on what I needed as he repeated his question two more times. When he didn't seem to, I pulled on his arm, drawing him close to me so he could see the tears running down my face.

Thomas sprang out of bed and rushed over to my side. He slipped his hand underneath my neck to support me. He cradled my head with one hand and with the other fed me a pain pill. As soon as he was confident I had it in my mouth, he picked up a bottle of water and guided it so I could take small sips. He held me until the pain seemed to subside, and he didn't let me go all night.

For the next few days I stayed home alone, texting my friend Sixto to distract me from the pain. The physical pain was nothing compared with the mental anguish of waiting for the biopsy results. No matter how many messages I sent him, Sixto answered and tried to give me hope that I'd be fine no matter what.

Finally, by the fourth day, when the pain had become bearable without my popping a Vicodin every four hours like clockwork, Dr. Biggs called.

"The pathologist examined your sample and found that you have a reactive lymph node that was benign, which means there is evidence of an autoimmune disease, but you probably don't have lymphoma."

Probably, I thought. *That's the best answer after all this time?*

"I'm going to see if she can retest the sample to give a better idea of what's really going on, but for now, I don't think there's anything to worry about," Dr. Biggs continued.

It's easy for him to say I shouldn't worry. I'm not about to wait for another cancer scare to figure out what's going on, I thought. *I've fucked around long enough. I keep saying I'm going to take action, but I've done almost nothing. Well, it's now or never, because the next trip to the hospital could be my last one.*

Chapter 17: The Agony of Defeat

The threat of cancer lit a fire under me. I wasn't certain I didn't want to die until I was faced with the prospect of not having a choice to live. Immediately after my biopsy, I was on the phone, fighting for my survival with new vigor.

"Dr. Thomas, I'm sorry to bother you, but I need a referral to a diagnostician, a person who specializes in strange medical cases, just like Dr. Gregory House from the television show. Does someone like that exist?" I asked.

"Those kinds of doctors do exist, but they're very hard to find," he replied. "I do know of one, whose nickname is Dr. Diagnosis."

"I hate that I have to ask, but please tell me this guy is covered by my medical plan."

"He is, but his waiting list is very long. Let me call to see if I can get you moved up," Dr. Thomas said. "Also, how are you doing since your surgery?"

"I'm okay. Rattled, but okay," I said, as my voice started trembling. "I really need to know why I'm like this. I can't keep just waiting for another cancer scare or stroke or something far worse."

"I know this has been a long journey for you, Nika."

"I hope it's almost over," I said.

By the time I arrived at Dr. Diagnosis's office that Thursday afternoon, the waiting room was full. I started to believe I was only bellyaching about my ailments when I saw the people there struggling just to move. Some patients had physical deformities. Others were in visible agony. I was fine—well, as long as I stayed medicated. Itchy armpits, dry mouth and eyes, stomach pains, fatigue, and a pocket full of pills seemed like nothing compared with what these other people were dealing with.

I was becoming increasingly unsure that I should even be at Dr. Diagnosis's office until I started wondering if the other patients had appeared more like me before whatever was wrong with them had progressed. I wondered if it was then that they had gone out of their way to find someone to solve their medical mystery, as I had done. My speculation evaporated as I grew more frustrated with the amount of time I had been waiting; it had already been nearly an hour and fifteen minutes.

"I'm on lunch break from work," I said to the receptionist filing her nails in front of me. "I've been waiting for the doctor for more than an hour. Do you know how much longer it will be?"

She barely looked up from what she was doing to respond, "You're next."

I know that, I thought. *I've watched just about everyone else in the place go in. Almost no one is left but me.*

I stomped back over to my seat, unsure if I should leave. The itching coming from the fresh scar on my neck reminded me exactly what I was there for and why I shouldn't let my temper get the best of me. I sat, tapping my feet and glaring over at the receptionist, for another ten minutes, before I heard, "Ms. Beamon. Sorry for the wait."

Dr. Diagnosis stood in the doorway of this tiny exam room, holding my file and summoning me forward. I angrily hustled over to him, brushing past him as I made my way into the room.

"What can I do for you?" he asked, with his back to me at his desk.

"I'm here because I thought you could help me," I replied. "I need a diagnosis, and I heard that's your specialty."

"It is, but I'm not sure I have any answers for you," he said. "I've examined your records and test results from your host of doctors, and it seems they ran the same tests I would have."

"So, what are you saying?" I snapped.

"I could order a CT scan, but I see here your medical company denied it once before."

"Without it you don't think you can figure out what's wrong with me?"

"Well, you know you have gastroesophageal reflux disease, polycystic ovarian syndrome, insulin resistance syndrome, nonalcoholic fatty liver disease, and lymphadenopathy. You are already being treated for all that."

"What about the twenty pounds I've lost, the night sweats, the dry mouth and eyes, and the extreme fatigue I feel?" I asked. "What explains all that?"

"Any combination of those conditions could explain it."

"So, that's it?"

"It's not that I don't believe something is wrong with you, Ms. Beamon," he said. "Clearly there is, but, short of a CT scan or an exploratory surgery, I don't think I'll be able to pin down one underlying condition."

"How much is a CT scan?"

"They can cost about two thousand dollars, so I doubt you want to pay for it out of pocket."

Does he think I can't pay for it because I am a single black woman? I thought. *Or is it that he doesn't think I deserve answers?*

My silence must have been a signal of my displeasure, because he said, "It's just that most people can't afford to pay that kind of money out of pocket."

"I understand exactly what you mean," I said sarcastically, as I began to pick up my jacket.

"Without the test, I don't see what else I can do for you. I'm a bit stuck."

"So, am I just supposed to keep waiting for another serious illness before you or any other doctor will help me?" I shouted, letting out all my pent-up frustration.

Seeming to have no reaction to my outburst, Dr. Diagnosis said, "I think you should keep seeing your doctors, keep a log of your symptoms, and call if something changes."

"That's it?" I asked again.

Dr. Diagnosis ignored my question and asked, "Are you still working?"

"Yes. Why?"

"Well, your condition doesn't seem to be debilitating or disabling, so I think you should just continue your medication, and you should be fine."

Fine? I thought. *Five specialists and a fistful of pills isn't fine. I guess it is to him, though, because he doesn't have to live this way.*

"I guess I was wrong about your being able to help me," I said, rising to my feet. I stuffed my arms into my jacket and headed for the door.

"Ms. Beamon, please take my card. If your symptoms get worse or there is anything I can do for you in the future, please give me a call."

I snatched the card from his hand and threw it into my pocket, knowing full well I never planned to call him again.

I need to find another doctor, I thought. *I'm not fine, and I don't want to accept that just because I can still function, I'm okay—that's BS.*

The moment I got back to my desk at work, I hit the Internet, searching for a real Dr. Diagnosis—one who would actually take the time to try to figure out what was wrong with me, and not just dismiss me.

I began by doing a Google search for the top doctors in New York. I didn't care whether the doctors accepted my medical plan or not; I just wanted the best. At the top of the results list was a *New York* magazine Best Doctors issue. I jotted down the names of several physicians whose specialties were both rheumatology and immunology. I figured most doctors I'd seen suspected I had some sort of autoimmune condition or chronic infection, so these contacts would be a good start. I didn't end my search there, though; I moved on to *U.S. News & World Report*'s Top Doctors list. It didn't take me long to notice that one female doctor was present on both lists, so she got an asterisk next to her name. Then I was on to Castle Connolly's America's Best Doctors directory. Once again, Dr.

Reed's name was there too. That entry pushed her to the top of my list.

Dr. Reed may be just what I've been looking for, I thought. *I just hope she'll take me on.*

Chapter 18: Should I Call You Dr. or Mrs. House?

I hate waiting, I thought as I sat in Dr. Reed's lobby. *I'm wasting whatever time I have left on this planet doing nothing but reading outdated magazines, staring at the clock on my phone, and scrolling through meaningless Facebook posts.*

"Ms. Beamon," the nurse's assistant said. "Can you follow me?"

I strolled past all the exam rooms wondering, *Where the hell am I going? I thought I was finally going to meet Dr. Reed; instead I'm headed to some back room.*

"Please have a seat," the nurse's aide continued. "I'm going to take your blood pressure and a few blood samples."

Well, at least I'm making some progress, I thought.

Once the nurse's aide finished, she sent me right back outside to the waiting area, where I remained for another half hour. An hour and fifteen minutes in, I was readying myself to get up and walk out, when my name was called again.

"Ms. Beamon, please go to exam room eight. The doctor will come in shortly," the nurse said.

This doctor better be worth the wait, I thought, as I sat on the roll of paper protecting the exam table. I began swinging my feet like an anxious child as I glanced around the room. I couldn't look more than a few inches in either direction without seeing a collection of plaques, each containing the cover of one of the magazines naming Dr. Reed top in her field.

"Ms. Beamon, I'm Dr. Reed," she said as she entered the room, extending her hand. The petite blonde looked as if she could have been some doctor's trophy wife, rather than the standout of her family. "You can have a seat in this chair right next to my desk."

I plopped down into the hard wooden seat and was immediately assaulted by questions from Dr. Reed. Instead of being overwhelmed, I was delighted.

"I've read your file, but I want you to tell me in your own words about your symptoms: What are they? When did they start? When did they get worse? How are you feeling now?" Dr. Reed asked in rapid succession.

She's actually taking the time to get to know me to try to figure out what's wrong with me, I thought. *I may have finally chosen the right doctor.*

I meticulously went through all of my aches, pains, pills, and procedures, leaving out none of the gory details from the past seventeen years, and concluding with my lymphadenectomy just a month prior.

"Along with your other symptoms, do your joints hurt? Are you constantly tired? Do you ever have dry mouth or dry eyes?"

"I do. How did you know?" I asked.

"Based on what I've seen from your records, your past test results, and your symptoms, I think I have a good idea of what's going on."

"Come again?" I exclaimed. "You think you know what's wrong with me?"

I wanted to hug her, lift her off the ground, and swing her around to show her how ecstatic I was that she had even an inkling of what had ailed me for so long.

"I'm going to run some blood tests to confirm my suspicions. I'd also like to get a CT of your pelvis and abdomen, with and without contrast. Have you had one?"

"No, my infectious-disease specialist tried to get it approved, but my health care company denied it twice. They said they needed further evidence of lymphoma, which is why she ordered it, or another qualifying reason."

"Well, if the blood test confirms that you have what I think, I'm certain I can get your insurer to pay for the test."

"If you really think I need it, I'm not opposed to paying for it out of pocket."

"I really think we can get it approved. In the meantime, I'm going to order a pelvic and abdominal ultrasound. Your health care provider should not have a problem with your getting that done. It's not as thorough as the CT scan."

"So, that's it?" I asked, as I collected my test referral forms and stood up, preparing to leave.

"For now, if I am right, there are some additional medications that can ease your symptoms."

"Not cure them?"

"There is no cure for most autoimmune conditions, including the one I think you have," Dr. Reed responded. "Some people get a lot of relief and can be pretty asymptomatic, but there is no actual cure. It also depends on the damage the chronic inflammation of your organs and pseudotumors throughout your body have caused."

"May I ask what you think I have?" I queried, anxiously awaiting her response.

"Let me write it down," she said.

She scribbled something small on a piece of paper bearing her name and slid it over to me as if she were bidding at a silent auction. I glanced down and saw a collection of letters and a number: *IgG4*.

"IgG4. What's that?" I asked.

"IgG4-related systemic disease is a chronic inflammation in the cells and connective tissue in multiple organs. It's often marked by elevated levels of immunoglobulin G or antibodies in your blood. IgG4 antibodies are the most important antibodies for fighting bacterial and viral infections. High levels of it are a sign of a long-term or chronic infection or an autoimmune disease. It can cause you to feel joint and body aches and pain, cause tumors to form throughout your body, and cause your lymph nodes to swell, and it damages organs like the liver and pancreas, which seems to be what's happening to you."

I didn't know what to make of the information Dr. Reed had given me; it was almost too much to process. I left her office bewildered by the possible diagnosis.

I always believed that when a doctor finally figured out what was wrong with me, it would be something curable or at least recognizable, I thought. *I'm not certain that anyone, including me, knows anything about this condition at all. I am some kind of genetic freak.*

To educate myself, I began googling IgG4-related systemic disease and found very little. Sure, a lot of scholarly papers on the disease had been published, but they didn't say much a lay person would understand. Frustrated, I reached out to my TV station's medical doctor for guidance.

"I don't know much about IgG4-related systemic disease, but there is one place that may be able to help," Dr. Patel said. "You should go to the National Institutes of Health website and look up their Office of Rare Diseases Research."

"What's that?"

"In 2008, the NIH started a department to collect data on rare conditions in the United States. They also have an undiagnosed-disease program; I actually did a story on it. If your doctor submits your medical records, this department will evaluate them. If you are among the fifty to one hundred people they select every year, their doctors will try to diagnose you," Dr. Patel continued.

"How come the dozens of doctors I've had over the years have never mentioned it?" I asked, starting to fume about the prospect that I could have had an answer about my condition before I had to have a lymph node removed.

"I don't know," she replied. "A lot of doctors aren't familiar with it or have a hard time admitting they don't know what's wrong with a patient."

"I thought a doctor's job was to save lives," I snapped. "If this will help them do it, then why not pass the information along?"

I stomped away from Dr. Patel and got on my computer straight away. I typed in the web address for the National Institutes of Health and discovered she was right. There it was, in black and white: a site devoted to bizarre medical cases like mine. IgG4 was listed as one of the diseases the NIH defined as rare, or affecting fewer than two hundred thousand people in the United States. Even more interesting were the sections on how to find an expert on your own to help, on research and clinical trials, and on other organizations of interest, one of which was NORD, the National Organization for Rare Disorders.

I didn't even know an organization like this existed, I thought, as I perused their website. From there, I clicked on the link for another nonprofit: In Need Of Diagnosis, Inc. What struck me the most about this site were the testimonials from people like me, desperate for anyone to help figure out what was ailing them. It was the first time in years I didn't feel so isolated, despite my anger at my doctors for not having steered me toward these sites sooner.

I logged off after taking notes on all the sites, should I ever need them again. I still wasn't sure I would, though, until Dr. Reed called about a week later.

"Hello, Nika speaking," I said, as I pushed the SPEAKER button on my cell phone while driving.

"Ms. Beamon, Dr. Reed here. How are you feeling?"

"About the same, thanks," I said as I navigated my car down the 495 Helix leading to the Lincoln Tunnel on my way to work.

"I got your test results back, and your G4 antibodies are high," said Dr. Reed.

"So, does that mean I have the condition you mentioned?"

"It appears so," she replied. "I also have some good news: your health plan approved the CT scan, so we can finally take a look at your organs to see what's going on. I suspect an inflamed pancreas is behind your dry mouth, and your inflamed liver explains your abdominal pain, but the test will confirm all that."

"So, what's the next step after the scan?"

"I'd like to avoid steroids, if possible, so I will have you continue the meds you are on and add a twice-daily anti-inflammatory drug given to lupus patients. It should reduce the swelling in your joints and organs and relieve some of your pain and the side effects of the condition."

"Okay," I said, as my voice started to crack.

"Great, so schedule the test, and I will see you in a couple of weeks."

As soon as she hung up, I dialed Thomas.

"Thomas, guess what?" I said, choking up as I spoke. "The doctor called, and she knows what's wrong with me. I can't believe it; I really can't. So many years, so much wondering, and someone finally knows."

I began bawling like a little kid, complete with clear snot streaming out of my nose.

"That's amazing, honey," Thomas replied. "Are you okay?"

"I don't know what I am. I waited so long for an answer. I've been through so much, and now I know all I needed was the right doctor."

"I know you've been through a lot, but at least you got an answer. Now we can get you healthy."

"The doctor says there is no cure but I can get better with more drugs."

"Well, that's a start."

"I know," I said. "I know it's silly I'm crying, but I'm overcome. I can barely think."

"I'm sure, honey. It's been a long journey."

My cell phone disconnected as soon as I reached the middle of the center tube of the tunnel. It freed me up to grab a tissue from my glove compartment and wipe my face; I didn't want to go into work with tearstains on my face. The fifteen minutes it took me to get from the other side of the tunnel to work gave me just enough time to compose myself and walk in as if nothing had changed, even though my world felt entirely different.

I couldn't get the doctor's call out of my mind, and it got me
thinking about whether that National Institutes of Health website I'd been on a week or so earlier had any other information that would help me. So I logged back on and went straight to the clinical-trials section. I plugged *IgG4* into the search column, and up popped several ongoing trials.

Wait, there are people trying to find a cure for people like me, I thought. *That's fantastic.*

I scanned through the list of studies to find the ones that were ongoing, then read the criteria.

Mass General in Boston has a clinical trial that sounds perfect. I wonder if I should apply for it and *allow myself to be a human guinea pig*, I thought. Then it hit me: *Why not? I've been one all these years. If I've learned nothing else, I know I'm going to have to fight to improve the quality of my life.*

Chapter 19: Not Lucky, but Blessed

Dr. Reed helped me get over feeling sorry for myself—about drawing the short straw in the genetic lottery. She prescribed drugs that helped decrease the inflammation in my body, thus restoring my energy and reducing my pain. A zest for life that had waned as my body deteriorated returned to me. I also began to understand that while I wasn't lucky when it came to my health, I was certainly blessed to be doing better.

I was also fortunate to have lived through so many close calls, to have had some doctors who bucked convention to try to solve my medical riddle, and to have been supported by family and friends when I couldn't do it for myself. Even more amazing, I had found a man who loved me in spite of it all.

These lessons really hit home for me when I noticed an AP alert come across the computer on my desk on May 4, 2012. I was slumped over, writhing with hunger pains because my new "lifesaving" medication made it difficult to eat, when I read, OBIT: ADAM YAUCH, DEAD AT 47.

No self-respecting child of the '80s—let alone a black child growing up in New York—could not know who Yauch was or not be aware of the group the Beastie Boys. Now, I'm no rap AFICIONADO, but I didn't need to be. The tracks from *Licensed to Ill* were constantly on the radio when I was younger—so much so that the lyrics to the Beastie Boys' songs are still stuck in my head today. The rhymes seeped into my consciousness and became part of the soundtrack to my youth. If I think hard right now, I bet even a stiff like me could spit a few verses.

Still, it wasn't Yauch's music that made word of his death stop me cold.

Forty-seven, I thought. *Not much older than I am.*

And it wasn't even Yauch's age alone that left me sitting in my cubicle with my mouth agape. It was that he died from cancer—specifically, cancer of the salivary gland that had spread to his lymph nodes.

I hobbled from my desk and ducked into the ladies' room, sick to my stomach; it was churning in a way that made me think I'd lose my breakfast at any moment. But the second I reached the bathroom, I knew I didn't need to enter a stall; I needed to splash water on my face and compose myself. As I shook my face off, like a dog getting the water out of his coat, I caught a quick look at myself in the mirror. I stopped and stared at my reflection, paying particularly close attention to the three-and-a-half-inch scar on my neck from the biopsy I'd had when my doctor suspected lymphoma.

I wonder if Adam went through the same wide-ranging sweep of emotions as I did when he first learned he might have cancer, I thought. *I wonder if he thought he was cured, and what he went through when he figured out that neither he nor his doctors would be able to stop its progress.*

I stood thinking about whether Yauch learned the hard way the lessons I'd come to know: that doctors don't know everything; that many physicians are at the mercy of health care companies and coverage limitations in terms of what tests they can perform and when they can be scheduled; that they sometimes hope you have something common, easy to treat, that doesn't require a lot of time or fights with insurers; and that they often miss symptoms and signs because a patient doesn't fit a common mold.

I was flooded with these thoughts as I rubbed my finger over the sensitive, raised scar resembling an earthworm on the right side of my neck. But my most prevalent thought was, *Why have I survived? Is it due to luck? Persistence? Preparation? Prayer?*

"Here I am," I mumbled, as I collected myself and meandered back over to my desk—back to work on Adam's obituary.

Ironically, I'm looking for video for a man who just a short time ago appeared to be much better off than I am, I thought. *He was rich, successful at his chosen profession, and well known, while I continue to toil in relative anonymity with mounting medical bills and failing health. Until today, if someone had asked me, I would've said Adam Yauch was the lucky one—certainly not me—but I was wrong. I am still here, and I am grateful.*

Resources

If I've learned anything from my years of seeking a correct diagnosis, it's that there are several basic steps that can help anyone who falls ill.

1. Get a yearly checkup.
2. Go to your doctor's office with a list of symptoms.
3. Write down your questions for your doctor. Don't hesitate to ask them.
4. If your doctor doesn't answer sufficiently, ask for a referral to another doctor. If you don't get one you like, there are several websites where you can search for one based on specialty, such as: www.castleconnolly.com/doctors/index.cfm http://health.usnews.com/top-doctors
5. When your doctor gives you test results or a diagnosis, look it up on sites like: http://symptoms.webmd.com/#./introView http://labtestsonline.org
6. Read all the instructions that come with your medications, including information about side effects. You can also look them up on sites like: www.drugs.com/sfx

7. If you feel like something is wrong with your body, continue to visit doctors until you get an answer. However, if it's clear that your doctors can't come up with a diagnosis, contact the National Institutes of Health's Office of Rare Diseases Research:

   National Center for Advancing Translational Sciences (NCATS)

   National Institutes of Health

   6701 Democracy Boulevard

   Suite 1001, MSC 4874

   Bethesda, MD 20892

   Phone: (301) 402-4336

   Fax: (301) 480-9655

   ordr@mail.nih.gov

   http://rarediseases.info.nih.gov

8. If your health plan refuses to pay for a test, appeal. Keep appealing until you get a yes. Contact your state's consumer assistance program. To find yours, go to www.healthcare.gov. You can look for your state in the Managing Your Insurance section.

9. If you need to talk about your symptoms or commune with other people you feel are suffering in the same manner, contact organizations that

deal with conditions similar to yours for help. The following is a list of them:

American Autoimmune Related Diseases Association
221000 Gralot Avenue
E. Detroit, MI 48021
or
750 17th Street, NW
Suite 1100
Washington, DC 20006

Autoimmune Information Network
This nonprofit organization helps patients and their families cope with the disabling effects of autoimmune disease through education and public awareness.
P.O. Box 4121
Brick, NJ 08723
(732) 664-9259
autoimmunehelp@aol.com
www.aininc.org

Bernie Mac Foundation
150 N. Michigan Avenue

Suite 2800

Chicago, IL 60601

Phone: (312) 291-4493

Fax: (312) 624-7701

info@berniemacfoundation.org

The Conill Institute for Chronic Illness

(215) 746-7267

info@conillinst.org

www.conillinst.org

IgG4-Related Systemic Disease Program

The Massachusetts General Hospital IgG4-Related Systemic Disease Program is a national leader in the areas of clinical care and research for this recently recognized condition.

http://www.massgeneral.org/rheumatology/services/treatmentprograms.aspx?id=1545

Immune Web

Created for people living with various immune system–related ailments, as well as for their significant others, family, friends, and medical care workers. This site provides lists of articles, books,

and other resources, as well as accounts of people's experiences.
www.immuneweb.org

Institute for Functional Medicine

3600 Cerrillos Road

Suite 712

Santa Fe, NM 87507

Phone: (505) 471-9020

Fax: (505) 424-3108

or

505 S. 336th Street

Suite 500

Federal Way, WA 98003

Phone: (800) 228-0622

Fax: (253) 661-8310

The Jennifer Jaff Center

195 Farmington Avenue

Suite 306

Farmington, CT 06032

patient_advocate@sbcglobal.net

www.thejenniferjaffcenter.org

National Organization for Rare Diseases

155 Kenosia Avenue

Danbury, CT 06810

or

1779 Massachusetts Avenue

Suite 500

Washington, DC 20036

Rheumatology Associates

Yawkey 2

55 Fruit Street

Boston, MA 02114

Phone: (617) 726-7938

Fax: (617) 643-1274

10. Have faith. *Never* lose faith!

Helpful Books

All in My Head: An Epic Quest to Cure an Unrelenting, Totally Unreasonable, and Only Slightly Enlightening Headache, by Paula Kamen

Living Well with Autoimmune Disease: What Your Doctor Doesn't Tell You . . . That You Need to Know, by Mary Shomon

Lupus: Everything You Need to Know (Answers to Your Most Common Questions About Systemic Lupus Erythematosus: Causes, Symptoms and Treatments), by Robert G. Lahita, MD, PhD

Lupus Q & A, by Robert G. Lahita, MD, PhD

Rheumatoid Arthritis: Everything You Need to Know, by Robert G. Lahita, MD, PhD

Systemic Lupus Erythematosus, **Fifth Edition, by Robert G. Lahita, MD, PhD**

The Arthritis Solution: The Newest Treatments to Help You Live Pain-Free, **by Robert G. Lahita, MD, PhD**

The Autoimmune Epidemic, **by Donna Jackson Nakazawa**

The Medical Science of House, M.D., by Andrew Holtz

The Sjögren's Syndrome Survival Guide, **by Teri Rumpf**

What Your Doctor May Not Tell You About Autoimmune Disorders: The Revolutionary, Drug-Free Treatments for Thyroid Disease, Lupus, MS, IBD, Chronic Fatigue, Rheumatoid Arthritis, and Other Diseases, **by Stephen Edelson**

Women and Autoimmune Disease: The Mysterious Ways Your Body Betrays Itself, by Robert G. Lahita, MD, PhD

Tips to compiling a complete medical record:

Get a copy of the summary or entry your doctor makes in your file after every visit

Request a copy of blood test results and all other test results after every visit, if applicable

Type or write a list of all of you doctors, complete with address and phone numbers

Type or write a list of your medications, including doses, purpose and pharmacy (quick tip: save the description page that comes with every prescription because all of this information is detailed on it)

Type or write a list of your emergency contacts (quick tip: if you have an iphone with a password, download an app that will allow first responders access to this list, if they need it. Also, keep a printed copy in your wallet and desk at work)

Type a list containing the name and address of your attorney, if you have one, who drafted your will, health proxy and/or power of attorney (give a copy to a trusted person and keep one at home)

Make sure a copy health proxy is easily accessible in your home and the people listed in it have a copy

Take advantage of the online portals being offered by a lot of doctors (store the passwords in your medical file

Take all of the above and place them in a pendaflex, home safe or some other spot where it can be located easily by someone you trust.

*A complete medical record will assist you in getting the best care should you need emergency care or can't speak for yourself. A recent study found 12 million Americans are misdiagnosed every year; that 1 in 20 patients.

<u>Tips to Ensuring You Get The Best Medical Care:</u>

Have a complete medical record

Research doctors/specialists treating your ailment/condition

Research test results and diagnoses on trusted websites

Always get a second, third opinion, if necessary

Keep a journal of your symptoms

Write down questions to ask your doctor and bring them with you

If you can't speak for yourself, bring someone with you to your doctor's appointments

If you can't get a diagnosis from your doctors, contact the office of rare diseases for assistance

Join organizations for your condition (it's a good place to gather information and network patients with similar symptoms)

Join a support group (it's a place to talk about your feelings and get additional information about treatments and doctors)

Five Things Chronically Ill People Should Make Sure They Have or Do To Ensure Peace of Mind:

Insurance: If possible you should purchase primary and supplemental medical care and prescription drugs coverage to minimize your bills. You should also purchase long term disability insurance. Life insurance is also essential to cover medical or any other bills you might leave behind.

Will: it's essential to make sure your loved ones won't have to fight for your assets while grieving your loss. It also allows you to establish trusts and other tax shelters to keep more of the money and property out of the grasp of tax collectors. Finally, it gives you a chance to leave behind a statement to your loved ones and to designate sentimental items you might want them to have.

Health Proxy: This document is essential to makes sure your wish about organ donation, resuscitation, and all aspects of your care are respected. It also lets medical professions know who you'd like to make decisions on your behalf if you cannot. It's also a document single people can use to give their significant other access to visit them in the hospital in areas like ICU only reserved for family or people in charge of your care.

Power Of Attorney: This document will immediately allow someone to take control of your finances, etc... if you become incapacitated. Once again, this is critical for single people because a battle can ensure over who should pay your bills or make decisions about your life.

Create a support network: collect a group of friends, co-workers, church members, family members, etc... who can assist you when you are not well. Try to keep the group large so you have a steady stream of visitors if you have a prolonged illness. It's also important so no one person gets burned out or overburdened.

Bonus Tip:

Be Honest: This seems like a bizarre entry but it's the most critical. Chronically ill individuals have to be honest with themselves about their
 illness so they can be proactive about their care, get their affairs in orders and inform their loved ones when they need help, company, or other support). They also need to make sure those around them are honest about being overwhelmed, emotionally drained, financial tapped, etc.. Chronically ill people also have to be honest with doctors about symptoms, poor care, and unanswered questions.

Five Tips for Someone Caring for a Chronically Ill Person:

Offer assistance: Sometimes it is best if you offer to run errands, bring a meal by, or stop by for a visit without being asked. It makes the sick person feel less guilty about asking constantly and less like a burden.

Rotate Care with someone else: Studies have shown caregivers also suffer physically and emotionally if they dedicate their lies to taking care of another person. So, it's important for you to have other people to step in when you are exhausted. You also need to make sure you get massages to relax, see your doctor regularly, and get plenty of rest and eat right.

Treat the person like a friend, not a patient: Make sure you remember to talk to your friend about something other than their care or illness; they're still a person who likes to joke, laugh, etc...

Pump up the positivity: keeping the spirits and morale high of the chronically ill person will help with their recovery.

Don't Preach: It's very tempting to pity a chronically ill person, often leading to the urge to tell them what to do, how to eat, when to sleep, what to take and how to lives their lives. Although, the "lectures" are an attempt to make sure the chronically ill person feels better, it actually accomplishes the opposite. It's okay to ask, even suggest, at times but less is definitely more.

Guide Questions for Misdiagnosed:

1. How common is misdiagnosis?

2. What should a person do if they believe they've been misdiagnosed?

3. Are there any tips people can follow to make sure they get the bets medical care?

4. Obamacare has been debated for the last few years, what are the advantages of the Affordable Health Care Act for chronically ill people?

5. What's the most common misperceptions about people with chronic illnesses?

6. Are there any tips for dating when you are sick and single?

7. What are some of the challenges to being sick and single?

8. Medical terms can be intimidating to most people, what should someone do if they don't understand what they're doctor is telling them?

9. How to make sure you get the answers from your doctors you really need?

10. How you can people be supportive to a chronically ill friend or relative?

11. What are five things chronically ill people need to know about taking care of themselves?

12. What are five steps chronically ill sick people need to take to make sure they're affairs are in order?

13. How important is faith in recovering from or living with illnesses?

Acknowledgements:

I would like to thank everyone who took the time to read an advance copy of my book and provided a blurb or support as I continued to forge forward.

To Rhonda McCollough, widow of Comedian Bernie Mac: I thank you for sharing your story with me about Bernard's harrowing journey. I hope to update this book one day soon so the world can know how much he was loved and laughed while fighting through pain.

To Richard Cohen: You are an inspiration to me. You reached out and took time for me even though we have never met. I am humbled and honored to have been able to have your read my work. I am even more touched at your generous nature; it allowed you to try to push me in the midst of your journey.

To Marya Hornbacher: We were strangers when I reached out to you and yet you didn't hesitate to show me kindness, spare time and energy to read my work and lend your praise. I'm grateful!

To Wes Moore: We are barely acquaintances, although I can say your family has been a blessing in my life. You greeted me with a smile when we met in person and made my heart smile with your words of praise. THANK YOU!

To Robert G. Lahita: I know you've truly chosen the right profession in life because you're understanding of the needs of the sickly is outstanding. The professional knowledge and feedback you shared is invaluable.

To Andrew Holtz: I thank you for reading my work and finding any comparison between it and the popular shows you've written about and shed light on for the public. I appreciate your willingness to help me.

To Paula Kaamen: You were one of the first authors to enthusiastically support my book and I am still choked up by your wonderful gesture.

To Shaniqua Seth: What can I say to you after all the great things you wrote about my journey in the book? All I can think of is thank you for all you've done and continue to do to make the lives of all women better.

To Nicoletta: Skoufalos: Your blog put me on the map and for that I am indebted to you.

When I began this book, I knew I wasn't just telling my story, I was sharing, at least part of the lives, of people I hold dear. Thank you all for seeing my vision and supporting it. My journey has been long but it has so been worth it because I was fortunate to have wonderful parents, Gloria and Randolph Beamon. I have amazing men as brothers: Randy and Taharka Beamon. One nephew who I am blessed to have watched grow up: Jeffrey Quinzon-Beamon.

The family I was born into isn't the only one I've lucky to have with me For more than 15 years, my co-workers at WABC-TV have been by my side. Here are just a few that stand out: Carmin Biggs, Lila Corn-Rosenwig, Kemberly Richardson, Sandra Bookman, Ken Rosato, Peter Kunz, David Evans, Janet Lawler, and too many more to mention by name. I love you all!

I would be remiss if I didn't mention my former classmates from Boston College, co-workers at ESPN Classic and WABU-TV in Boston.

I'll just list a few other people by name without whom my life would not have been worth living: Sixto Reynoso, Alexis Keim, Karen Santo, Kiada Morgane, Matthew Harrington, Diane Elliott, Marc VanSchaick, Cylysce Martinez, Monica Eaton, and Branden and Melvina Cobb.

Additionally, I want to offer special thanks to my agent Chelcee Johns at Serendipity Literary. If you hadn't seen the potential in my early draft, I might not have taken the steps to craft it into a book I can be proud of and one I'm willing to share with the world. Thank you to Regina Brooks, Nadeen Gayle and everyone else at Serendipity Literary for your counsel, as well.

Finally, to anyone not mentioned by name who has played a significant role in my life and recovery. THANK YOU! LOVE YOU!

Author Biography:

Nika C. Beamon is a TV News Writer/Producer in New York City. She pursued a B.A. in Sociology and a B.A. in Communications at Boston College in Massachusetts. She's been a journalist for twenty years. She has won numerous awards throughout her career, including a Peabody Awards for ABC News' coverage of the September 11th attacks.

In 2009, Beamon published her first non-fiction book, I Didn't Work This Hard Just to Get Married: Successful, Singe Black Women Speak Out. Her first mystery novel, Dark Recesses, was released in 2000. Her second mystery novel, Eyewitness, was published in 2002.

Contact: Http:www.nikabeamon.com

Made in the USA
Charleston, SC
30 October 2014